GEOLOGY
of the KELOWNA AREA
and ORIGIN of the OKANAGAN VALLEY
BRITISH COLUMBIA

Murray A. Roed

with contributions from

Don A. Dobson, George Ewonus, John D. Greenough,

Brian Hughes, H.A. (Herb) Luttmerding,

Peter Peto, Norman Williams

KELOWNA GEOLOGY COMMITTEE

Kelowna Geology Committee
c/o Geology Department
Okanagan University College
3333 College Way
Kelowna, British Columbia V1V 1V7

The Publisher: Kelowna Geology Committee

Canadian Cataloguing-in-Publication Data
Roed. M.A., 1937-
Geology of the Kelowna Area and the Origin of the Okanagan Valley, British Columbia.
Includes bibliographical references and index
1. Geology–British Columbia–Okanagan Valley
2. Geology–British Columbia–Kelowna Region
I. Dobson, Don (Don A.) II. Kelowna Geology Committee III. Title
QE187.R64 1995   557.11'5   C95-900622-2

ISBN 0-9699795-0-9

Book Layout and Cover Design: Jack Thompson
Printing and Production by:
Ehmann Printing Ltd.
470 Cawston Avenue
Kelowna, British Columbia V1V 6Y9

Front Cover Photograph: M.A. Roed
Pinnacle Rock, westerly view, Gallagher's Canyon
Back Cover Photograph: M.A. Roed
West Kettle Columns, Okanagan Falls Forestry Road
Graphics and Sketches: Hanny Muggeridge, M.A. Roed

Kelowna Geology Committee:
    Don A. Dobson, George Ewonus, John D. Greenough, Brian Hughes,
Murray A. Roed, Dave Schneider, Paul Tomelin, Norm Williams.

    Distributed by: Foxview Management Limited,
1365 Crawford Road,
Kelowna, B.C. V1Y 8R3,
Phone: (604) 764-2600;
°Fax: (604) 764-2605.

Cost: $19.95C

Sponsors

$5000 - 10,000
GEOLOGICAL FOUNDATION OF CANADA

$1000 - 3000
BHP MINERALS CANADA LTD.
BRENDA MINES LTD.
CENTRAL OKANAGAN FOUNDATION
CENTRAL OKANAGAN REGIONAL DISTRICT
FRIENDS OF THE ENVIRONMENT FOUNDATION
GEOLOGY DEPARTMENT, OKANAGAN UNIVERSITY COLLEGE
GEOTERRAIN CONSULTANTS
INTERIOR TESTING SERVICES LTD.
OKANAGAN SCIENCE, TECHNOLOGY AND INNOVATION COUNCIL
SUNSET RANCH GOLF DEVELOPMENTS LTD.

$500 - 1000
DIA-MET MINERALS LTD.
MIDLAND-WALWYN LTD.
RIVERSIDE FOREST PRODUCTS LTD.

$100 - 300
CHEMAC ENVIRONMENTAL SERVICES
DOBSON ENGINEERING LTD.
EBA ENGINEERING LTD.
FDN FOUNDATION ENGINEERING LTD.
GOLDER ASSOCIATES
GORMAN BROS. LUMBER LTD.
GRAND OKANAGAN LAKEFRONT RESORT
HENDERSON FORESTRY CONSULTING
P. JENSEN & ASSOCIATES ENGINEERING LTD.
PROTECH CONSULTANTS LTD.
REID CROWTHER & PARTNERS LTD.
RHF SYSTEMS LTD.
URBAN SYSTEMS LTD.
WILLIAM AND GLORIA KAUFMAN

$100
AIR HART
GLOBAL TERRAIN MANAGEMENT INC.
HOWARD CAMPBELL
KELOWNA GRIZZLIES BASEBALL LTD.
KELOWNA MOHAWK/CJ WALKER ENTERPRISES LTD.
MOULD ENGINEERING LTD.
ROBERT C. GORE
UMA ENGINEERING

THE GEOLOGY OF THE KELOWNA AREA

AND THE ORIGIN OF THE OKANAGAN VALLEY

BRITISH COLUMBIA

Acknowledgements

Encouragement to produce this book was received from the staff of the Kelowna Museum, numerous members of the Okanagan Naturalists Club and the Kelowna Branch of the Okanagan Historical Society. Thanks are due to the Rutland Water District staff who supplied timely data for the Rutland aquifer, and the Ministry of Transportation and Highways in Kamloops for providing drilling information from each end of the Kelowna floating bridge.

A list of donors is given at the front of the book. Without these generous funds, this book could not have been published in its present form. The largest donation was from the Geological Foundation of the Geological Association of Canada, and we thank them for their consideration and patience.

Special acknowledgement is due to Dr. John D. Greenough, Geology Department, Okanagan University College. Not only did he embrace this project and encourage its completion, John conducted a revision of the manuscript, is a contributing author of several chapters, provided photographs and produced a bedrock field trip guide included here as an Appendix. John acted as Chairman of the Kelowna Geology Committee, handled all administrative matters, and dedicated a portion of his research budget to prepare illustrations for the book.

The cooperation of the Accounting Department of the Okanagan University College in Kelowna is also gratefully acknowledged. The Grants-In-Aid Committee of the College contributed toward drafting expenses through a grant to Dr. Greenough. Many of the maps and drawings in the book have been drawn by Hanny Muggeridge, who also reviewed the manuscript and provided editorial advice. Word processing duties were fulfilled by Debra M. Roed who also tolerated the paraphernalia of such a project in her home. Herb Luttmerding greatly assisted by conducting a final reading of the manuscript.

Research for the book was assisted through discussions with Dirk Templemann-Kluit, Robert J. Fulton, and John J. Clague of the Geological Survey of Canada, and Neil Church of the Geological Survey Branch of the British Columbia Ministry of Mines and Petroleum Resources who also reviewed a portion of the manuscript and contributed information. The cooperation of Glenda Malcolm of Brenda Mines Ltd. was greatly appreciated.

Last but not least, this book would not have been possible without the written contributions of Don Dobson, George Ewonus, John Greenough, Brian Hughes, Herb Luttmerding, Peter Peto and Norman Williams, and the help of Dave Schneider of Rutland Senior Secondary School, and Paul Tomelin of the Kelowna Prospectors Club; thanks for your time everyone.

Foreword

Travel through ancient history and discover the origin of the Okanagan Valley, view volcanic landforms formed when the valley experienced mountain building forces sixty million years ago, envision the landscape 10,000 years ago when glacial Lake Penticton stretched for two hundred kilometres or more, and discover the beginnings of present day Okanagan Lake and the area in the vicinity of the City of Kelowna. These are just a few of the fascinating subjects in this account of the Kelowna area geology. This book is designed for the local lay-person, visitors, and as a resource guide for educators. It focuses on the geologic landmarks of the area and how geology has influenced the evolution of the present landscape and touches the lives of everyone. It is hoped that the extensive information provided on the natural history of the Okanagan Valley in British Columbia will enrich and inspire the reader.

The prime objective is to enhance awareness of the substantial impact geology has on the environmental resources of the area, and how these resources contribute to the long-term integrity of the Okanagan Valley. Ultimately, the goal is to generate a higher level of appreciation of the natural features and heritage, stimulate increased use of earth sciences, engineering and archeology in future planning, and provide a needed record of the geology of this part of western Canada.

Any profit from sales will be utilized for a college or university scholarship, for geological displays in the Kelowna Museum and for interpretive displays elsewhere.

An extensive list of References is given alphabetically at the end of the book. A specific source of information in the text of the book is shown in parenthesis by author(s) and date. The reference list does not include every publication on the geology of the Okanagan. The writers beg the pardon of colleagues for any unintentional omissions.

Field trips given in Appendix A and B offer, respectively, a general sight-seeing tour and a specific tour which visits localities representing products of ancient mountain building events. Both facilitate self-guided tours to some spectacular natural features. A summary of "geofacts" for Kelowna is given in Appendix C, and definitions of a number of technical terms are included in Appendix D at the back of the book. A subject index is given in Appendix E.

The discerning reader may note that some explanations of the geology are repeated. This reflects the intention to make each section of the book a stand-alone product as much as possible.

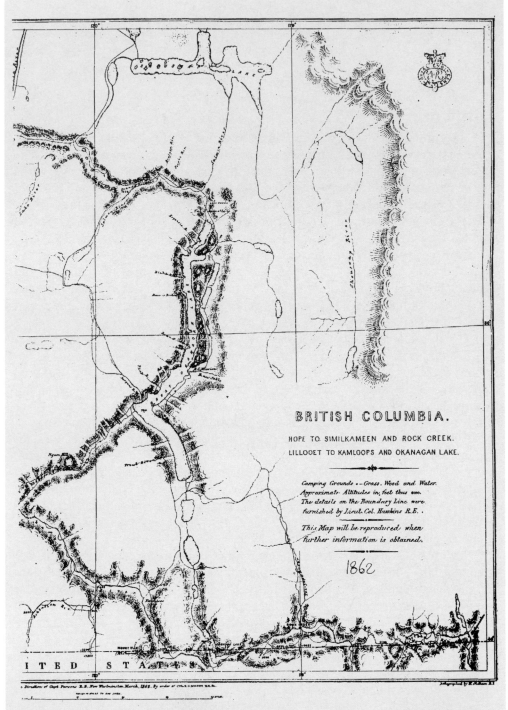

BRITISH COLUMBIA.

HOPE TO. SIMILKAMEEN AND ROCK CREEK.

LILLOOET TO KAMLOOPS AND OKANAGAN LAKE.

Camping Grounds • – Grass, Wood and Water.
Approximate Altitudes in feet thus 100.
The details on the Boundary Line were
furnished by Lieut. Col. Hawkins R.E. •

This Map will be reproduced when
further information is obtained.

1862

ITED   STATES

*A portion of the earliest map of the interior of British Columbia, drawn by
A.C. Anderson who did the work between 1832 and 1851.*

CHAPTER 1

HISTORY OF GEOLOGICAL STUDIES IN THE OKANAGAN VALLEY AT KELOWNA

The first geologist to visit the Okanagan Valley was George Mercer Dawson in 1877. The scope of his observations while travelling by foot, canoe and horseback was phenomenal. He commented on or described in detail every major geologic feature visible in the valley. Dawson was a Nova Scotia born scientist educated at McGill University. He joined the Geological Survey of Canada in 1872 and was first assigned to a joint British and American survey of the International Boundary. In 1875 he obtained an appointment to undertake a geological survey of British Columbia which led to a life-long devotion. Dawson arrived at Kelowna on July 3, 1877, and the next day visited the placer mines at Mission Creek (Cole and Lockner, 1989, p. 342). The creek below Gallagher's Canyon had been mined for gold for at least sixteen years. Dawson reported that coarse gold of two to three ounces per day per man was still being recovered there at that time, mainly from McDougall's claim (Dawson, 1879, p. 157b).

Plate 1: Dr. George Mercer Dawson, centre and standing, with his field crew at Fort MacLeod, Alberta, in 1879.

Courtesy of the Geological Survey of Canada (photo number GSC 311).

George Dawson born in 1849 was the son of Sir William Dawson, a noted geologist and principal of McGill University. Dawson has been called the "little giant" of Canadian geology. His achievements are even more remarkable given his physical condition. He was no bigger than a boy of 12, had weak lungs, and a bent and hunched back, all effects of a childhood illness. Yet in 1887, for example, he traversed over 164,000 square kilometres of northern British Columbia, and then explored the Yukon nearly a decade before the Klondike gold rush of 1896. He was an avid collector of plants and flowers, and described all of those found along his wide ranging routes. He discovered numerous fossil localities, and had a particular interest in the language and culture of North American Indians. In 1895 Dawson took over the Director's chair of the Geological Survey of Canada. He suddenly died in 1901.

Geological investigation in the Kelowna area appears to have been largely absent during the next fifty years. Various geologists with the British Columbia Department of Mines periodically examined scattered mine workings, but no formal studies were conducted. Exceptions to this include a study by L. Reinecke (1915) on the ore deposits at Beaverdell in the early 1900's, and a treatise that focused attention on the physiographic or geomorphic aspect of the Okanagan Highland. C.E. Cairnes of the Geological Survey of Canada began a study of mineral resources of the northern Okanagan Valley in 1930. He then systematically began mapping the Kettle River map sheet which today is part of the Penticton map sheet number 82E of the National Topographic System where Kelowna is situated. Cairnes emphasized the mineral deposits of the region and also produced the first bedrock geologic map that included the Kelowna area (Cairnes, 1937). The early thirties witnessed considerable excitement about an alleged oil discovery near the mouth of Mission Creek at Kelowna. A summary is given by a skeptical Cairnes.

Cairnes' map remained the only geologic map of the area until H.G. Little spent five months in 1958 and 1959 revising Cairnes' work. Little's work was probably initiated as a result of geologic mapping in the Vernon area by H.M.A. Rice in 1945 and 1946 which was continued by A.G. Jones from 1947 to 1951 (Jones, 1959). These studies were greatly facilitated by access provided by the Hope-Princeton Highway opened in 1944. Railroad access via the Kettle Valley Railway had been continuous since 1916.

Other studies in the Okanagan between 1930 and 1950 focused on the glacial deposits of the region. Inspired by Dawson's original descriptions of ice-rafted deposits and his final and correct conclusion that the area was affected by extensive ice sheets, numerous scientists began to decipher the surficial deposits and origin of the present day landforms. The "white silts" described by Dawson are exposed in cliffs along Okanagan Lake and have long attracted the curiosity of geological scientists (Flint, 1935; Meyer and Yenne, 1940; Mathews, 1944), and still continue to do so (Shaw and Archer, 1979).

Despite widespread interest and importance of surficial geology, or glacial geology, it was as late as 1962 before Hugh W. Nasmith published maps showing the distribution of these deposits in the southern Okanagan Valley (Nasmith, 1962). Nasmith's maps remain widely used even though they are reconnaissance in nature with a scale of 1:250,000. Agricultural soil scientists have since mapped the soils of the Kelowna area in considerable detail (e.g. U. Wittneben, 1986), but little has been added to the glacial geology inventory since Nasmith. An exception to this is Stuart S. Holland's synthesis of British Columbia's landforms which is still the main authority on the physiographic divisions of the Okanagan Valley area (Holland, 1964).

Beginning about 1960, an explosion of geological work began in British Columbia that in most cases relates only in a general way to the Okanagan. Groundwater resources were inventoried for the Okanagan Basin Study during the early 1970's. This included the first seismic profile across the valley north of Vernon. Soils maps of most agricultural areas were produced during the 1960's. Maps of the terrain and soils for the Canada Land Inventory project were completed during the 1970's. Recent specific and/or comprehensive studies for the Kelowna area are restricted to bedrock geology open file maps by Templemann-Kluit (1989), and an inventory of mineral occurrences by Meyers and Taylor (1989).

Volcanic rocks of Tertiary age in the Kelowna area have been of particular interest to Neil Church of the British Columbia Geological Survey (Church, 1980 and 1981). Church's maps are the only detailed bedrock geology maps ever published for the Kelowna area. W.H. Mathews of the University of British Columbia has recently studied plateau volcanics of late Tertiary age in uplands east of Kelowna (Mathews, 1988).

Other contemporary geologists who have made major recent contributions to the geology of the Okanagan Valley are Wheeler of the Geological Survey Canada, editor of a new bedrock geology map of the Cordillera, Okulitich for regional bedrock mapping in the North Okanagan, Parish and colleagues for their work on age dating and structural evolution of the Shuswap Terrane, Monger for his work on plate tectonics, Christopher for work on uranium and Beaverdell silver, Fulton for key discoveries related to the early glacial history of the area, and Eyles *et al* (1990) for an illuminating look at the sediment fill of Okanagan Lake.

CHAPTER 2

GEOLOGIC TIME

Geologists estimate that the earth formed about 4.6 billion years ago. The oldest rocks preserved on earth are about 4.0 billion years old. They mark the beginning of the Precambrian Eon which extends to 570 million years ago when fossilized animal life forms become abundant. Most of the rock material comprising the continents formed at this time. Rocks perhaps as old as 2.0 billion years old occur in Kelowna generally east of Okanagan Lake.

GEOLOGIC TIME INTERVALS			Millions of Years Ago
ERA	PERIOD	EPOCH	
CENOZOIC	QUATERNARY	Holocene	(Recent) 0.01
CENOZOIC	QUATERNARY	Pleistocene	2.0
CENOZOIC	TERTIARY	Pliocene	5.0
CENOZOIC	TERTIARY	Miocene	24
CENOZOIC	TERTIARY	Oligocene	37
CENOZOIC	TERTIARY	Eocene	58
CENOZOIC	TERTIARY	Paleocene	66
MESOZOIC	CRETACEOUS		144
MESOZOIC	JURASSIC		208
MESOZOIC	TRIASSIC		245
PALEOZOIC	PERMIAN		286
PALEOZOIC	PENNSYLVANIAN		320
PALEOZOIC	MISSISSIPPIAN		360
PALEOZOIC	DEVONIAN		405
PALEOZOIC	SILURIAN		438
PALEOZOIC	ORDOVICIAN		505
PALEOZOIC	CAMBRIAN		570
PRECAMBRIAN			birth of planet 4600

Figure 1: Geologic time divisions.

The last 570 million years of geologic time forms the Phanerozoic Eon. It is formally divided into three major Eras, from oldest to youngest the Paleozoic, Mesozoic and Cenozoic (Figure 1). These Eras are divided into periods (e.g. Tertiary) and the Periods into Epochs (e.g. Eocene).

During the Paleozoic Era, from 570 to 245 million years ago, a great diversity of marine life and environments waxed and waned across the Earth. Evidence of this Era of time in the Kelowna area is largely absent.

The Mesozoic Era spans from 245 to 66 million years ago and represents a time of major change in life forms and geologic events on Earth. For example,

AGE

Figure 2: Geologic Column of the Kelowna Area

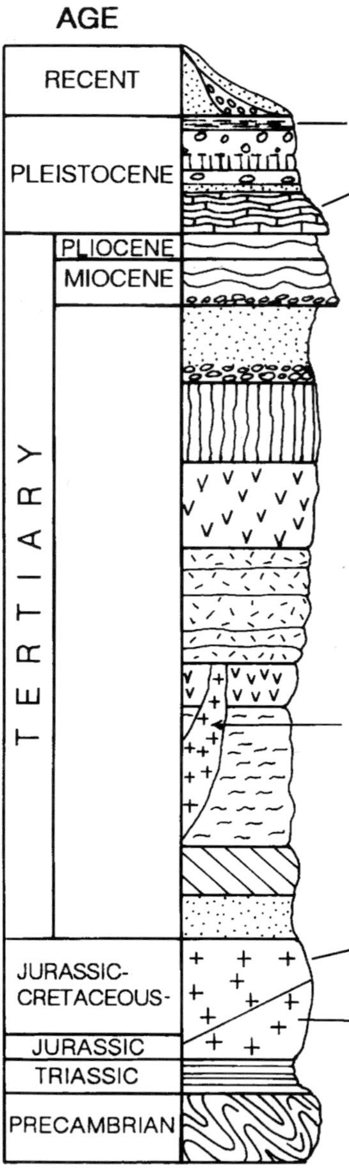

RECENT DEPOSITS, Sand and gravel in streams and alluvial fans, colluvium, landslides, organic.

GLACIAL DEPOSITS, Fraser Glacier, Glacial Lake Penticton, Okanagan Centre drift.

LAMBLY CREEK BASALT, 30 - 60 m thick, 0.762 million years old, bench along hilltop west end of Okanagan bridge, a valley basalt.

PLATEAU BASALT, Lava up to 340 m thick, Kallis and King Edward Formations, underlying gravel in channels, Chilcotin Group.

WHITE LAKE FORMATION, Sandstone, conglomerate, siltstone, plant fossils, 425 m thick.

MARAMA FORMATION, Dacite, breccia, Mt. Boucherie volcanic dome.

MARRON FORMATION,
Nimpit Lake Member, Mt. Knox, Layer Cake Hill, trachyte lava flow, 250 m thick.

Kitley Lake Member, Trachyte lava with phenocrysts, 360 m thick, base of Mt. Knox.
Trepanier rhyolite, pink, white, green volcanic flows.
Andesite lava, breccia, 150 m thick.

CORYELL INTRUSION, Granite and syenite, feeder to Kitley Lake flows, 46.8 million years old.

KETTLE RIVER FORMATION, Dacite, obsidian, quartz veins, 300 m thick, Black Knight Mtn., Mt. Dilworth.

Rhyolite breccia and flow banded lava.

Siltstone, sandstone, carbonaceous seams.

OKANAGAN BATHOLITH, Granitic rocks.

NELSON PLUTONIC ROCKS, Granite, granodiorite.

Slate, phyllite, argillite, quartzite, limestone, greenstone, fossiliferous, Transported Quesnellia Terrane.

MONASHEE GNEISS, Metamorphic rocks of the Shuswap Terrane, 2.0 billion years old or more.

AGE column labels (top to bottom): RECENT, PLEISTOCENE, PLIOCENE, MIOCENE, TERTIARY, JURASSIC-CRETACEOUS-, JURASSIC, TRIASSIC, PRECAMBRIAN

dinosaurs flourished in the swamplands of the Alberta and Saskatchewan plains, and ancient continents began to break up to form their present configuration. During the time of the dinosaurs Kelowna was the site of mountain building with rocks being folded, broken, uplifted, transported, heated and injected with molten rock from deep in the Earth.

The Cenozoic spans from 66 million years ago to the present. During this time interval which includes the locally important Tertiary Period many of the visible geologic features in the Kelowna area were formed. The Ice Age (the Pleistocene Epoch) occurred near the end of the Cenozoic, and we live in the Holocene or Recent Epoch of the Cenozoic Era.

GEOLOGIC COLUMN OF THE KELOWNA AREA

The main geologic deposits and their respective ages that can be found in the Kelowna area are shown in a geologic column of Figure 2 compiled from Templemann-Kluit (1989) and Church (1980). From oldest to youngest these are:

PRECAMBRIAN...Monashee Gneiss or Shuswap Rocks

The Monashee Gneiss may represent the oldest rocks in British Columbia at 2.0 billion years. These rocks originally formed the Pacific edge of a very old continental nucleus of North America known as the Precambrian Shield. For much of their existence these rocks were deeply buried (10-40 kilometres) and several times subjected to great heat and pressure during mountain building events. As a result the original chemical elements of the rocks have been repeatedly rearranged to form new minerals producing the banded metamorphic rock known as gneiss. These rocks comprise a belt of highlands in central British Columbia extending from the Canada/United States border to Valemount, near Jasper National Park. How these deeply buried rocks came to occupy a substantial surface area around Kelowna is of profound interest to geoscientists as discussed in Chapter Four.

PALEOZOIC

Although limestones and other rocks of Paleozoic age occur at Vernon and Penticton they do not occur in the vicinity of Kelowna. They have been completely eroded away leaving a gap in the rock record. Such a gap is known as an unconformity.

MESOZOIC

The Mesozoic Era at Kelowna is represented by marine siltstone and shale of Triassic age, and by granitic intrusive rocks of Jurassic to Cretaceous age. The Kelowna area during this time was affected by a number of globally significant geologic events that scientists piece together by studying the region as a whole and interpreting their observations in a plate tectonic context (see Chapter Four).

CENOZOIC

Many geologic features in the Kelowna area formed during the Cenozoic Era which started 66 million years ago. During the first period of the Cenozoic, the Tertiary Period, Kelowna was often volcanically active. Most local surficial deposits formed during the Quaternary Period, which begins with the Pleistocene Epoch (Ice Age), and ends with the Holocene Epoch (the last 10,000 years).

Tertiary

Rocks of Tertiary age are widespread in the Kelowna area and are primarily volcanic in origin. The rocks make up the Kettle River, Marron and Marama Formations which belong to the Penticton Group (Church, 1980 and 1981). Well known landmarks such as Dilworth Mountain, Knox Mountain, Layer Cake Hill, Mount Boucherie, and Black Knight Mountain formed from local volcanic activity fifty to sixty million years ago. When volcanism ceased river delta and stream deposits of the White Lake Formation partially buried the previous volcanic landscape.

The youngest Tertiary deposits are basalt lava flows of the Chilcotin Group which poured out across uplands and flooded ancient river valleys. Today the lava flows, commonly with underlying river gravels, form topographic high points due to their resistance to erosion. Radiometric dating suggests at least two episodes of volcanic activity (Mathews, 1988). Flows belonging to the King Edward Formation erupted eleven to twenty million years ago and occur on the upland north of Mission Creek toward Vernon. Kallis Formation flows erupted less than seven million years ago and can be found in the Big White Mountain and Hydraulic Lake areas.

Quaternary

Various deposits and landforms were produced during several glaciations and interglacial events of the Pleistocene Epoch, the first part of the Quaternary, beginning perhaps two million years ago. Minor volcanic activity is also known from this time interval. The Lambly Creek basalt on the west side of Okanagan Lake erupted 760,000 years ago. Also, some plateau basalts in the Hydraulic Lakes area east of Kelowna poured out of fissures one to three million years ago.

At the beginning of the Holocene Epoch, the last part of the Quaternary, 10,000 years ago, a huge glacial lake occupied the valley. When it drained sediments that had accumulated at its edge were exposed and eroded forming "benches" or "silt bluffs" characteristic of the Kelowna and Penticton landscape.

CHAPTER 3

PHYSIOGRAPHIC DIVISIONS

The landscapes of southern British Columbia are defined by major physiographic divisions which include the Coast Mountains, Thompson Plateau, Okanagan Highland, Shuswap Highland, Monashee Mountains, Selkirk Mountains, and far to the east the Purcell Mountains (Figure 3). Striking linear lake-filled valleys are common to most of these regions, an impressive example being the Okanagan Valley.

The Okanagan Valley at Kelowna transects a portion of an upland called the Thompson Plateau on the west and part of the Okanagan Highland to the east.

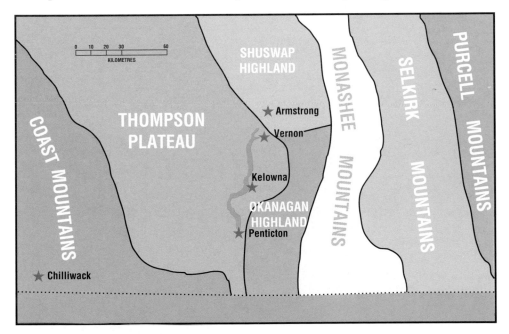

Figure 3: Physiographic Divisions

The region occupies the southern portion of the Interior Mountain System commonly referred to as the Intermontane Belt. The origin of these physiographic units is broadly described below.

THOMPSON PLATEAU

Volcanic and sedimentary rocks underlying most of the Thompson Plateau at Kelowna represent exotic terrane (they originated somewhere in the Pacific) that was added to the side of the North American continent as a result of North American and Pacific plate convergence during the Mesozoic (see Chapter Four). Later this terrane was pervasively intruded by magmas now forming granitic rocks. The bedrock making up the Thompson Plateau began to take its present physiographic or topographic form in late Eocene and early Oligocene times. Much of the interior of British Columbia was then uplifted in response to the gradual rise of the Rocky Mountains to the east and subduction of the Pacific Plate at the Continental Margin to the west. The plateau's broad rolling to gently sloping high level "plains" today resulted from extensive erosion of this uplift and represent an ancient "peneplained" surface. Remnants of these upland surfaces are now bordered by prominent valleys over 1000 metres deep. The valleys formed by gradual stream dissection of the ancient peneplain in the late Tertiary or early Quaternary Periods.

Near the end of the prolonged period of Thompson Plateau uplift, volcanic activity began in the interior of British Columbia. Volcanism commenced as early

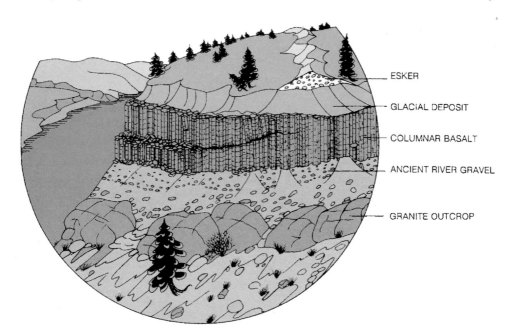

ESKER

GLACIAL DEPOSIT

COLUMNAR BASALT

ANCIENT RIVER GRAVEL

GRANITE OUTCROP

Figure 4: Typical Escarpment: Thompson Plateau

as twenty million years ago and peaked ten to fifteen million years ago. The highly fluid basaltic lavas flowed out over many parts of the vast pre-existing peneplain topography forming "plateau basalts" referred to as the Chilcotin Volcanics. The lavas spread out in thin sheets, travelling for great distances along flat-bottomed valleys of the ancient peneplain drainage system. These basalt flows tend to exaggerate the present day plateau surface of the Thompson Plateau in places.

The Chilcotin lava obliterated a regional river system that had developed on the peneplain of central British Columbia. Details of the drainage pattern are not known but geologists do know that a province-wide drainage system existed that was far different from what exists today. Even the mighty Fraser River drained northward during this time. Remnants of this river system exist today as gravel deposits preserved below plateau basalts. A geologic profile of the plateau basalts and river gravels typically exposed along valleys walls cutting through the Thompson Plateau is illustrated in Figure 4.

OKANAGAN HIGHLAND

Rolling to somewhat rugged mountains of the Okanagan Highland flank the Thompson Plateau to the east (Figure 3). The area is dominated by Precambrian metamorphic rocks known as Shuswap or Monashee Gneiss. These rocks have been involved in several mountain building events during which they were buried, heated, compressed, and changed in appearance. At the end of the Precambrian, the breakup of a very old continent placed these rocks at the edge of the North American continent. During the Eocene and Oligocene Epochs the rocks were thrust up from the west along a great fault located along Okanagan Lake at Kelowna. The Okanagan Highland represents the roots of an ancient mountain system that emerged during the Tertiary Period (Chapter Four).

The Okanagan Highland also includes Jurassic to Cretaceous granite and diorite igneous rocks referred to as the Okanagan Batholith and Middle Jurassic Nelson Plutonic Rocks. These rocks intrude the Shuswap rocks south of Beaverdell and in Okanagan Mountain Park. Heat from another substantial group of granitic rocks of Tertiary age referred to as the Valhalla Intrusives has affected this area and has reset the "radiometric clock" of the Monashee Gneiss to reflect an early Tertiary period of metamorphism (Mathews, 1988).

Other Okanagan Highland rocks include minor patches of Upper Paleozoic to Lower Mesozoic Pacific ocean volcanic and sedimentary rocks of the Nicola Group that were "sutured" to and thrust onto the North American continent during the Mesozoic. Several volcanic calderas of Eocene age occur partly in the Okanagan Highland. One is the Kelowna basin, another occurs at Summerland, a third at Penticton and a fourth at Vernon.

Like the Thompson Plateau, the Okanagan Highland is locally capped by late Tertiary, Chilcotin Group plateau basalts. At some locations sand and gravel deposits up to 50 metres thick and 100 to 300 metres wide underlie the basalts.

The sedimentology, distribution, orientation, and elevation (1000 meters above the present Okanagan Valley bottom) of these gravel deposits give evidence for a high energy drainage system bearing no relationship to the present or earliest Quaternary (pre-Ice Age) drainage patterns. Excellent examples of these ancient channel deposits can be viewed in the Grizzly Upland along King Edward Creek southeast of Vernon, east of Oyama, along West Kettle River on the way to Big White Mountain, and in some exposures along the Kettle Valley Railway above Kelowna.

EFFECTS OF GLACIATION

The Okanagan Highland experienced the same general uplift and erosion as the Thompson Plateau and both were heavily abraded by at least two and perhaps four Cordilleran glaciers during the Pleistocene (Chapter Five). Uplands today are mantled with a thin glacial moraine related to the melting and retreat of the last Cordilleran ice sheet, the Fraser Glacier.

Valleys in the Okanagan Highland and Thompson Plateau are dominated by interbedded moraine and outwash deposits in well formed terraces. Some valleys, notably Mission Creek and Okanagan Lake valley, show extensive silt bluffs and linear terraces composed of silt, clay and sand related to glacial lake sedimentation.

Several spectacular rock-rimmed canyons with tumbling mountain streams mark the western part of the Okanagan Highland east of Kelowna. Examples include KLO Creek, Myra Canyon and Bellevue Creek. The Crawford Trail and portions of the Kettle Valley Railway offer excellent opportunities to view representative geologic features of the Okanagan Highland. These canyons and many present valleys were formed approximately ten to twelve thousand years ago as a result of deep erosion from meltwater during deglaciation. Mission Creek and the upstream portion of Gallaghers Canyon (Plate 2) offer the best opportunities to view the effect of the extensive erosion that occurred.

Plate 2: A near vertical cliff eroded by Mission Creek since the end of glaciation is one of the many geologic features of the Gallagher's Canyon area in Kelowna.

CHAPTER 4

GEOLOGICAL HISTORY OF BEDROCK IN THE KELOWNA AREA

John D. Greenough and Murray A. Roed

The principal geological events that formed the bedrock geology of the Okanagan Valley at Kelowna are summarized in this chapter. Discussion is restricted to pre-glacial events. A generalized bedrock geology map of the Kelowna area appears in Figure 5.

PLATE TECTONICS OF THE OKANAGAN

Over the last thirty years the theory of plate tectonics has revolutionized geologic thought. According to this theory a rigid outer layer of the earth, composed in part of the earth's crust, is divided into plates. Like ice on a pond these plates "float" on a partially-molten or semi-solid portion of the mantle. The mantle moves (convects) and the overlying plates are carried along as if on a conveyor belt. In places, particularly at ridges in the ocean basins, plates move away from one another forming new basaltic ocean floor. Where plates collide, ocean floor may be pushed beneath other ocean floor or below continental crust. This process, known as subduction, results in volcanoes (e.g. Cascades and Aleutians), folding, faulting and metamorphism. In short, mountain building occurs. It is also possible for two continental plates to collide (e.g. Himilayas) and for plates to slide past one another (e.g. San Andreas fault).

British Columbia is part of the North American Plate and the Pacific Ocean forms the Pacific Plate (Figure 6). Over the past 200 million years, subduction of ocean floor below North America has periodically resulted in portions of the Pacific Plate being successively "pasted" to the side of the continent. The result is a series of northerly trending terranes of foreign or exotic origin. Some originated in the southwest Pacific whereas others have always been part of the North American continent. The accreted (added) terranes account for four-fifths of the width of the Canadian Cordilleran mountain range and perhaps fifty percent of its volume.

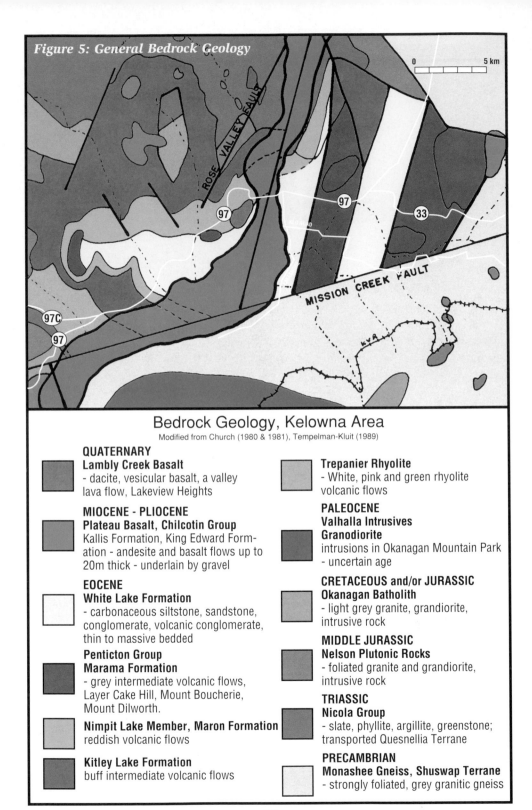

Figure 5: General Bedrock Geology

0   5 km

Bedrock Geology, Kelowna Area
Modified from Church (1980 & 1981), Tempelman-Kluit (1989)

QUATERNARY
Lambly Creek Basalt
- dacite, vesicular basalt, a valley
lava flow, Lakeview Heights

MIOCENE - PLIOCENE
Plateau Basalt, Chilcotin Group
Kallis Formation, King Edward Formation - andesite and basalt flows up to
20m thick - underlain by gravel

EOCENE
White Lake Formation
- carbonaceous siltstone, sandstone,
conglomerate, volcanic conglomerate,
thin to massive bedded

Penticton Group
Marama Formation
- grey intermediate volcanic flows,
Layer Cake Hill, Mount Boucherie,
Mount Dilworth.

Nimpit Lake Member, Maron Formation
reddish volcanic flows

Kitley Lake Formation
buff intermediate volcanic flows

Trepanier Rhyolite
- White, pink and green rhyolite
volcanic flows

PALEOCENE
Valhalla Intrusives
Granodiorite
intrusions in Okanagan Mountain Park
- uncertain age

CRETACEOUS and/or JURASSIC
Okanagan Batholith
- light grey granite, grandiorite,
intrusive rock

MIDDLE JURASSIC
Nelson Plutonic Rocks
- foliated granite and grandiorite,
intrusive rock

TRIASSIC
Nicola Group
- slate, phyllite, argillite, greenstone;
transported Quesnellia Terrane

PRECAMBRIAN
Monashee Gneiss, Shuswap Terrane
- strongly foliated, grey granitic gneiss

28

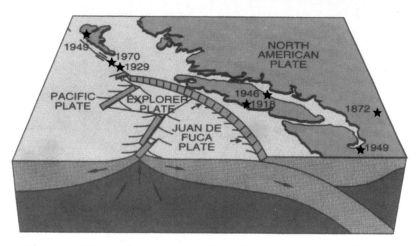

Figure 6: Simplified cross-section of southwestern British Columbia illustrates the Juan de Fuca and Explorer plates sliding beneath the North American plate off the west coast of Vancouver Island. Dates refer to major earthquakes.

Because of a gradual northwestern continental drift, the Kelowna area as recently as 25 million years ago was 400 to 500 kilometres further south of its present latitude. The climate was distinctly tropical, with rainfall in the order of 700 to 1000 centimetres per year, compared to the present 55 centimetres for the Okanagan watershed.

Transported Terrane

Current theories suggest that some of the terranes were actually thrust up onto the land and "transported" for many hundreds of kilometres (Figure 7). Other "terrane" was subducted (sucked down) beneath the continent and remelted with the water-saturated molten material rising to form the granitic rocks of the Coast Range, and other plutons such as the Okanagan Batholith.

The Okanagan surface has been affected by what is known as Quesnellia Terrane. This terrane represents a thick sedimentary and volcanic bedrock assemblage originally deposited in an island arc volcanic environment somewhere in the Pacific Ocean Basin. The terrane was "accreted" to the North American Plate during a collision sometime during the Jurassic Period starting 200 million years ago. The terrane was thrust over existing land and subsequently greatly modified by further mountain building forces, igneous intrusion, volcanic eruptions and by extensive uplift and erosion culminating in the Ice Age of the Quaternary. As a result, only a few remnants of Quesnellia Terrane exist in the Kelowna area.

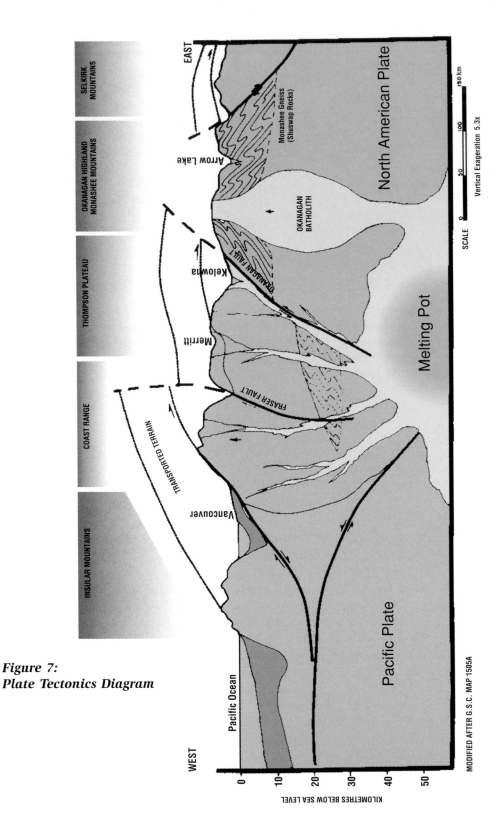

Figure 7:
Plate Tectonics Diagram

UPLIFT OF THE SHUSWAP TERRANE AT KELOWNA

Uplift of the Shuswap Terrane and Monashee Gneiss was a major event in the Okanagan and for British Columbia as a whole. This period of mountain building is referred to as the Columbian Orogeny.

As described previously Monashee gneisses of the Okanagan Highland represent rocks that were deeply buried when Quesnellia Terrane was thrust over and accreted to the edge of continental North America. Perhaps during Cretaceous time the Highland began to rise. At the same time extension caused major portions of the accreted Quesnellia Terrane to begin sliding off of the central rising mass. This westward sliding, presumably along the Okanagan Fault (see below), combined with erosion of Quesnellia Terrane rocks has served to bring Monashee gneisses of the Shuswap Terrane, once buried ten to forty kilometres, to the surface. This tectonic history is illustrated in Figure 8.

THE OKANAGAN FAULT

The Okanagan fault is a major zone of displacement in southern British Columbia. It has been determined by geophysical studies to be at least twenty kilometres deep. The fault is part of a system of north trending faults that can be traced for much of the length of the province. This discovery has relegated the Okanagan fault to the status of one of British Columbia's largest earth structures. Its influence on the geologic development of this part of the province has been profound.

The Okanagan fault played an important role in plate movements by acting as a major zone of rupture that allowed the final thrusting of the Shuswap Terrane up to the east as much as ten kilometres. The fault can be traced for at least 200 kilometres and closely follows the Okanagan Valley. In places the fault diverges from the trend of Okanagan Lake, notably where it coincides with Kalamalka Lake, and at the intersection between Mission Creek valley and Okanagan Lake at Kelowna. Here it appears that the fault has been displaced by an east-west trending fault. This second fault is likely responsible for the huge bend in Lake Okanagan, the so-called "knee" of the lake. Some details of the deformation along this fault can be seen in Gallagher's Canyon (Plate 3).

The Okanagan fault became most active in the Eocene Period (approximately sixty million years ago) and probably created a rugged landscape not unlike the Great Rift Valley of Africa.

Initial extension and movement on the fault likely coincided with the inception of Eocene volcanic activity that produced calderas at Penticton, Summerland, Kelowna, Vernon and other locations in the interior of the province.

EARLY TERTIARY VOLCANICS

Active volcanoes and large rivers dominated the rift-valley landscape of the Okanagan during the Eocene Epoch, 50 to 60 million years ago. The rock record

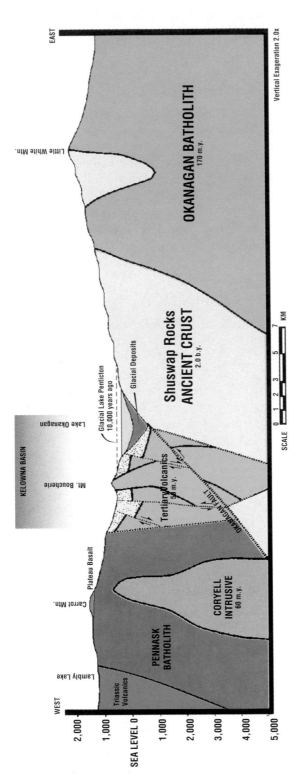

Figure 8: Cross section through Kelowna Basin showing the general distribution of the main rock types and examples of the main faults. Dashed lines are faults or breaks along which movement (arrows show relative direction) has taken place in the past.

Shuswap Rocks are composed of the Monashee Gneiss. The Coryell Intrusive and the Okanagan and Pennask Batholiths are composed of granite, diorite and syenite. Volcanics in the faulted Kelowna Basin include trachyte, andesite, basalt and

others which belong to the Kettle River Formation. The uppermost shaded unit is the White Lake Formation composed of siltstone, sandstone and conglomerate with coal layers and abundant plant fossils.

indicates that the volcanoes produced both lava flows and ash deposits not unlike the Cascade volcanoes Mount St. Helens and Mount Baker. Magma (molten rock) building these volcanoes had intermediate to high concentrations of silicon, an element that makes magma thick and sticky, and the volcano potentially explosive. A typical volcano went through one or more cone building stages during which both lava flows and ash deposits were repeatedly produced. Then, after a period of dormancy during which gases built up in the underlying magma chamber, a catastrophic eruption blasted away much of the volcano leaving behind a large bowl-shaped depression known as a caldera. Subsequent volcanism and stream activity served to fill the caldera with more lava flows, ash deposits and

Plate 3: A northerly view across Mission Creek valley at Gallagher's Canyon reveals a series of overturned folds (dashed lines) in sandstone of the White Lake Formation. The volcanic rocks of Layer Cake Hill just to the east (right) appear to have been thrust westward causing these spectacular folds. These northerly trending folds have been cut by substantial movement along a major easterly trending fault, the Mission Creek fault (forming the "knee" of Okanagan Lake). The Mission Creek fault apparently offsets the Okanagan fault zone.

volcanic-rich sediments. During the cone-building stage a hazard produced by the damp climate of the time was that snow built up on the peak of the volcano. Sudden melting during an eruption like the 1980 event at Mt. St. Helens yielded mudflows on the flanks referred to by geologists as lahars. Lahars cause extensive floods and widespread erosion, and may result in large volumes of sediment that choke drainage ways many kilometres downstream. Considering the volcanic threats, the propensity for flooding from abundant precipitation and the likelihood of earthquakes caused by movement on the Okanagan fault, Kelowna was a geologically hazardous spot during the Eocene!

An Early Tertiary River

Gradually volcanism waned in the valley. The region was subjected to sedimentary infilling caused by the development of a huge river system that deposited sediments of the White Lake Formation. Thick deposits of silt, sand, gravel and volcanic debris were deposited into the Kelowna basin partly burying the rugged volcanic terrain. Today this event can be envisioned at Boucherie Mountain where conglomerate and sandstone envelopes the base of the mountain (Plate 4).

This sedimentary event witnessed the emergence of forests that struggled to - develop in the flood prone margins of the Kelowna basin. Evidence of this

Plate 4: A northwesterly view along Okanagan Lake from Lakeshore Drive in Kelowna illustrating the envelopment of Mount Boucherie by the White Lake Formation forming a terrace-like landform at the base of the mountain.

ancient forest can be seen in thin coal beds preserved in the White Lake Formation exposed along Highway 97 near Westbank (See Hardrock Trail, Appendix B, Stop 4, and number 21 in Figure 19). Fossil trees occur in an almost upright position, as if they were suddenly buried, and many sandstone beds contain well preserved plant fragments. These rocks outcrop in many places around Kelowna such as beside Mission Creek

in Gallagher's Canyon, along Boucherie Road, in Glen Canyon Regional

Plate 5: Glen Canyon Regional Park displays many characteristics of the White Lake Formation. Along the picturesque Powers Creek here, sheer cliffs up to 100 metres high expose sandstone and conglomerate of the formation that have been eroded firstly by huge volumes of meltwater and then by the present creek which is still actively eroding its channel.

Park bordering Powers Creek, and along the western shore of Okanagan Lake south of the bridge (Plate 5).

Following deposition of the White Lake Formation the Kelowna area underwent a prolonged period of regional uplift, folding and faulting. The Okanagan region was subject to squeezing forces possibly related to the rise of the Rocky Mountains during Oligocene and early Miocene time from about 30 to 24 million years ago. Thus the older Eocene volcanic rocks and related sediments were folded and faulted. As explained above, good examples of the results of these mountain building forces can be viewed in Scenic Canyon Regional Park (Gallagher's Canyon) where sandstone of the White Lake Formation displays steeply upturned and even overturned beds (Plates 3 and 18).

This is when the Thompson Plateau and Okanagan Highland began to be eroded into a peneplain. The mountainous highland first became a major watershed that witnessed widespread erosion. One result was deposition of extensive deposits of sand and gravel that blanketed much of the foothills and adjacent plains of Alberta, 500 kilometres away. This activity ceased only when the Rockies began to rise in earnest by which time the Thompson Plateau and similar highlands in central British Columbia had been reduced to a broad peneplain with low relief.

A Late Tertiary River System

Prior to Miocene-Pliocene volcanic events in British Columbia a late Tertiary regional river system developed in central British Columbia, as mentioned in Chapter Two. Numerous examples of this river system occur in the Kelowna area. The associated sand and gravel deposits have been mined for their placer gold content. Gold tends to be concentrated at the base of the deposits where streams eroded into the underlying bedrock. The sand and gravel deposits of the ancient

Plate 6: A southerly view from the Kelowna Floating Bridge shows an escarpment along Lakeview Heights which is formed from the Lambly Creek valley basalt.

drainage system also became hosts for uranium deposits (see Chapter Eleven). Uranium-bearing groundwater percolated through faults and fractures in the underlying bedrock and deposited its uranium when it encountered the near-surface chemical conditions of the river gravels. Subsequent basaltic lava flows of Miocene to Pliocene age have not only acted to preserve the river sediments, they form a protective cap on the uranium precipitated in the gravels. At least one potentially mineable uranium deposit is known in the area.

LATE TERTIARY PLATEAU VOLCANISM

A prolonged period of basaltic volcanism began in the interior of British Columbia approximately 20 million years ago and resulted in the formation of the

Chilcotin Group plateau lavas that act as erosion-resistant caps on many hills in the Thompson Plateau and Okanagan Highland. Unlike the explosive Eocene volcanism where distinct volcanic edifices developed, the Chilcotin basalts passively emanated from long cracks or fissures that opened up in the crust. These highly fluid basaltic lavas spread out over the interior plateau and flowed down any river valleys or depressions existing at the time. The basalts remain relatively flat lying having been extruded after the cessation of tectonic forces that folded and faulted the early Tertiary rocks. Time-equivalent plateau lavas covering a similar area to that of the Chilcotin Group occur over the Columbia Plateau in neighbouring Washington State. Curiously, the American basalts are world famous but few geologists outside of British Columbia have heard of the Chilcotin Basalts!

In the Kelowna area, where streams and glaciers have eroded through the plateau basalt sequence a conspicuous, steep scarp has developed (Figure 4). Up to thirty individual basaltic flows occur near Kelowna in the area of Daves Creek. Individual flows are thin, and the total stratigraphic thickness of the basaltic flows rarely exceeds 100 metres. One of the most striking sections through the basalts occurs along the West Kettle River valley just south of the

Plate 7: This is a northerly view of vesicular basalt which makes up the Lambly Creek basalt forming Lakeview Escarpment.

Big White access road (photo on back of book cover). At least three basalt lava flows are exposed for over one kilometre along a forestry access road (West Kettle Columns in Figure 35). These basalts display spectacular pillar-like structures called columnar joints which develop when lava shrinks and fractures into vertical columns during cooling. They overlie a sand and gravel deposit, an example of stream activity just prior to the plateau basalt event.

A VALLEY BASALT EVENT

The last volcanic event to affect the Kelowna area is only 762,000 years old (Middle Pleistocene age). It is a valley basalt called the Lambly Creek basalt. It flowed twenty-five kilometres from a source north of Lambly Lake, down Lambly (Bear) Creek, and into the Okanagan Valley (Figure 5). It is preserved as a lava bench on the west side of the lake near the Okanagan Bridge and below the Lakeview Heights residential area, here referred to as the Lakeview Escarpment (Plates 6 and 7).

This valley basalt gives some idea of the topography in the area three quarters of a million years ago, and supports the belief that at least some of the tributary valleys were partly developed by that time.

The Lambly Creek basalt shows chemical similarities to the Chilcotin Group basalts. This reminds us that Chilcotin volcanic activity has probably not ended in the interior of British Columbia. Fortunately, the probability of an eruption during our life time appears extremely small.

SUMMARY

It is clear from this brief description of the volcanic history of the Kelowna area that the interior part of British Columbia has been geologically active for at least fifty million years. Total uplift in the Coast Range Mountains to the west is in the order of four kilometres in the last ten million years. It follows that there was extensive erosion in the region during this prolonged period of uplift. Erosion is one reason why there are many gaps in the geologic record in the Kelowna area, compared to other areas of the world. A sequence of diagrams in Figure 9 summarizes the main events.

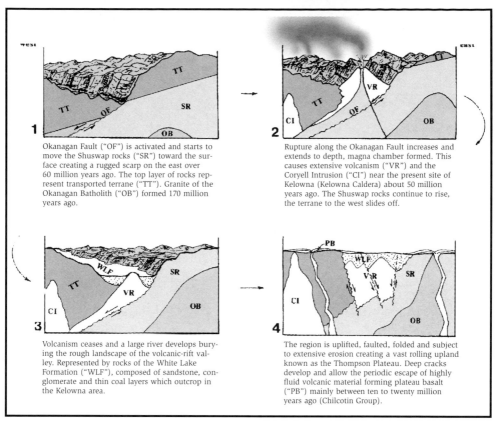

west   east

1 Okanagan Fault ("OF") is activated and starts to move the Shuswap rocks ("SR") toward the surface creating a rugged scarp on the east over 60 million years ago. The top layer of rocks represent transported terrane ("TT"). Granite of the Okanagan Batholith ("OB") formed 170 million years ago.

2 Rupture along the Okanagan Fault increases and extends to depth, magma chamber formed. This causes extensive volcanism ("VR") and the Coryell Intrusion ("CI") near the present site of Kelowna (Kelowna Caldera) about 50 million years ago. The Shuswap rocks continue to rise, the terrane to the west slides off.

3 Volcanism ceases and a large river develops burying the rough landscape of the volcanic-rift valley. Represented by rocks of the White Lake Formation ("WLF"), composed of sandstone, conglomerate and thin coal layers which outcrop in the Kelowna area.

4 The region is uplifted, faulted, folded and subject to extensive erosion creating a vast rolling upland known as the Thompson Plateau. Deep cracks develop and allow the periodic escape of highly fluid volcanic material forming plateau basalt ("PB") mainly between ten to twenty million years ago (Chilcotin Group).

Figure 9: Summary of Tertiary Geologic History at Kelowna.

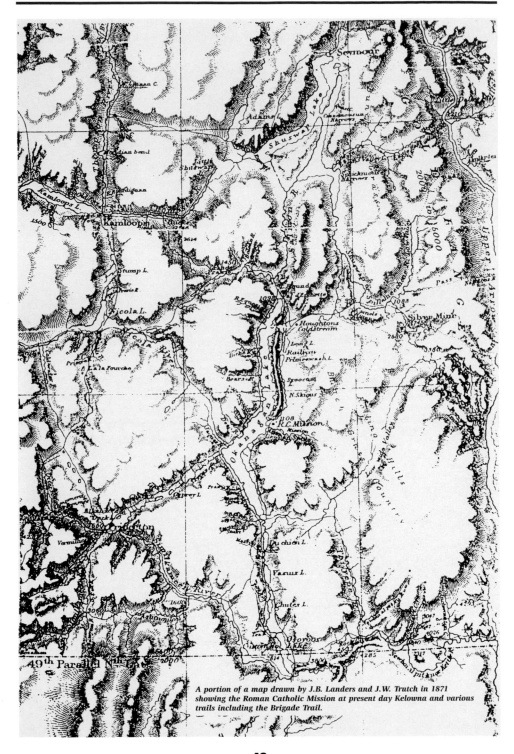

A portion of a map drawn by J.B. Landers and J.W. Trutch in 1871 showing the Roman Catholic Mission at present day Kelowna and various trails including the Brigade Trail.

CHAPTER 5

THE ICE AGE AT KELOWNA

The continued uplift of the region and the initial erosion of the present valleys down through the adjacent uplands to the end of Tertiary time combined with a gradual cooling of the climate set the stage for another dramatic geologic event, the Ice Age. This is the Pleistocene Epoch and it began approximately 1.6 million years ago. At first ice began accumulating at topographic high points and began to flow under the influence of gravity. The tongues of ice filled the valleys and coalesced in the larger valleys. Finally ice overtopped the valleys and spread out onto highlands. Glacial build-up reached its maximum when all of the ice accumulation areas merged. At this time, the Cordilleran Ice Sheet was formed and covered the entire province. From space, it probably looked like a vast brilliant blueish and white lobate collage marked by widely spaced, gently sloping dome-like mounds marking regional ice accumulation centres (Figure 10). Only the very highest peaks projected above the ice as nunataks.

To the east, along the Rocky Mountain Foothills in Alberta, the Athabasca lobe of the Cordilleran Ice Sheet merged with the Continental Ice Sheet and they flowed south together for several hundred kilometres into the United States. In the west, ice flowed out of the Cordillera, traversed the Continental Shelf and calved into deep water of the Pacific Ocean.

Most of the ice moving through the Okanagan originated in a major accumulation zone about 800 kilometres (500 miles) to the north in the northern Selkirk Mountains. Glacial ice flowing over the southern interior terminated in broad lobes that covered large parts of Idaho, Montana and Washington. These lobes are here referred to as the Columbia, Kootenay, Okanagan and Fraser lobes.

The ice sheet was 1000 to 3000 metres thick over much of the Interior of British Columbia. The most recent glacier at Kelowna may have been 3000 metres thick along the centre of the valley of Okanagan Lake. It flowed to the south and southeast as indicated by striae on bedrock in the area. Large boulders here and there known as erratics (Plate 8) attest to erosional power of the ice.

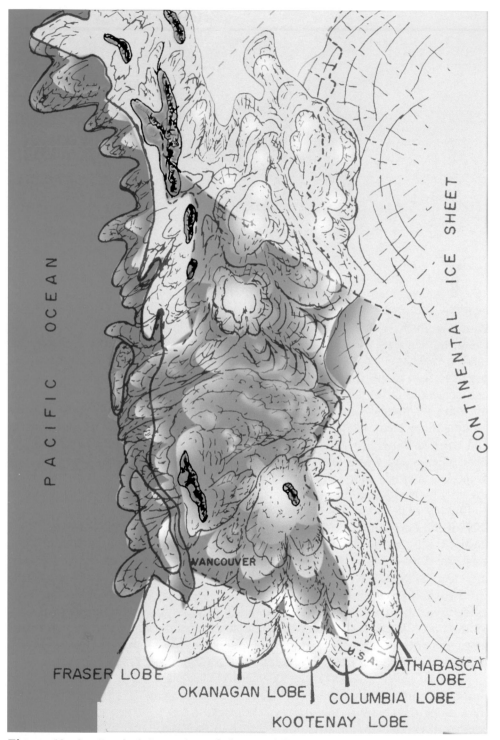

PACIFIC OCEAN

CONTINENTAL ICE SHEET

VANCOUVER

U.S.A.

FRASER LOBE

OKANAGAN LOBE

COLUMBIA LOBE

ATHABASCA LOBE

KOOTENAY LOBE

Figure 10: An "artistic" version of the Cordilleran Ice sheet from space.

Multiple Glaciations

There have been at least four intervals of Cordilleran ice build-up each separated by an

Plate 8: This large boulder of gneiss in Mission Creek valley is an example of an erratic. The rock was plucked from bedrock by a glacier and carried to its present spot where it was deposited when the ice melted.

interglacial period when the climate was warm and ice melted. However, according to Don Easterbrook, working in the State of Washington, at least six glaciations of the Cordilleran Ice Sheet entered the state from British Columbia during the Pleistocene Period. Canadian geoscientists (Fulton *et al*, 1992) have uncovered evidence of similar multiple glaciations at a locality near Merritt. Generally, in British Columbia, only the last two glaciations are known in any detail. The older is referred to as the Okanagan Centre Glaciation, and the younger as the Fraser Glaciation.

The Okanagan Centre Glaciation

Three kilometres south of Okanagan Centre (Figure 11) a sequence of glacial and nonglacial sediments ninety-eight metres thick is exposed in a gully (Figure 12) on the east side of the road. Fulton and Smith (1978) of the Geological Survey of Canada determined that they represent the last two major glacial advances (25,000 and 50,000 years

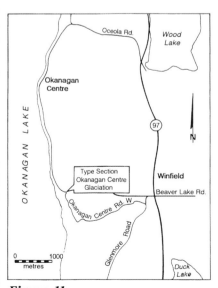

Figure 11

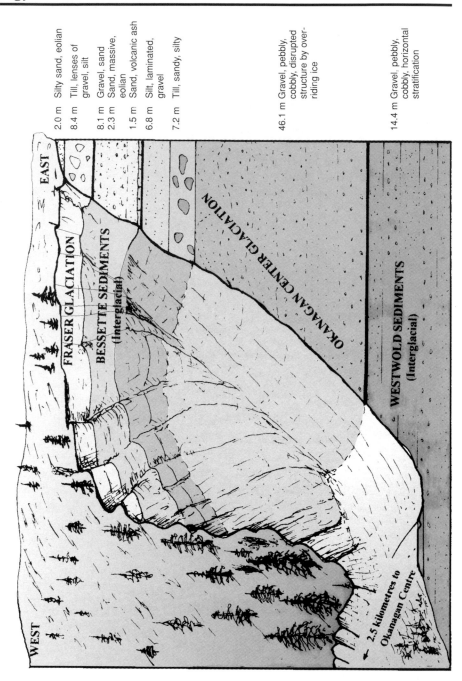

LITHOLOGY

2.0 m Silty sand, eolian

8.4 m Till, lenses of gravel, silt

8.1 m Gravel, sand

2.3 m Sand, massive, eolian

1.5 m Sand, volcanic ash

6.8 m Silt, laminated, gravel

7.2 m Till, sandy, silty

46.1 m Gravel, pebbly, cobbly, disrupted structure by over-riding ice

14.4 m Gravel, pebbly, cobbly, horizontal stratification

EAST

WEST

FRASER GLACIATION

BESSETTE SEDIMENTS (Interglacial)

OKANAGAN CENTER GLACIATION

WESTWOLD SEDIMENTS (Interglacial)

2.5 kilometres to Okanagan Centre

Figure 12: This gully along Okanagan Centre Road exposes one of the best sections revealing the variety of glacial deposits formed in the last 100,000 years in British Columbia.

ago) separated by a non-glacial interval, and an older Interglacial interval (100,000 years old).

The deposit that is laid down directly when glacier ice melts is called till (Plate 14). The till of the Okanagan Centre Glaciation is underlain by a series of glacial lake deposits, sand, gravel of glacial and fluvial origin and beach deposits referred to as the Westwold Sediments. Fossils recovered from these deposits at Westwold, B.C., include plant fragments, mollusk shells, bison bones, fish, beetles, and rodents suggesting a warm climate (Fulton and Smith, 1978) during a 100,000 year old Interglacial period in the Okanagan.

The till of the Okanagan Centre Glaciation is overlain by another series of sediments representing a regional period of nonglacial activity referred to as the Olympia Nonglacial Interval. These sediments were formed in many valleys after the ice of the Okanagan Centre Glaciation had melted. They are known as the Bessette Sediments and are exposed in Bessette Creek near Lumby where they are 22 metres thick and consist of interbedded fluvial gravel, sand and silt containing plant remains and at least two layers of volcanic ash. These deposits are overlain by till and sediment related to the most recent Cordilleran glaciation called the Fraser Glaciation.

Fraser Glaciation

The best known glaciation in British Columbia is the Fraser Glaciation because its deposits form much of the present surface terrain of the Province. In many localities only one till, representing one ice advance, occurs but in some places at least two tills occur which means that there were at least two advances of the Fraser Glacier. The Fraser Glacier completely engulfed British Columbia as recently as 19,000 years ago following an ice build-up that began about 25,000 years ago due to climatic change. Exactly what produced the climatic changes that caused the Ice Age is still an unsolved mystery but many theories exist.

Fraser Glaciation deposits consist of till that mantles most of the terrain today, outwash deposits of various sorts, late Pleistocene-earliest Holocene glacial lake deposits, and areas of bare bedrock that have been molded or scraped by ice, or eroded by meltwater. A variety of these deposits and the landforms produced occur near the major centres of Vernon, Kelowna and Penticton as summarized in the surficial geology map of Figure 13.

Glacial Lake Penticton

Approximately 10,000 years ago the lobe of the Fraser Glacier that occupied the Okanagan Valley formed an ice dam near Okanagan Falls south of Penticton as it melted. Meltwater flowing into the valley ponded behind this dam. This formed a lake much larger and deeper than Okanagan Lake known as Lake Penticton. Sediments deposited in this lake basin form the high, silt bluffs up and down the valley. These silt bluffs and associated terraces impart much of the beauty to the landscape for which the Okanagan is famous. Lake Penticton reached a maximum elevation of 457 metres, over 100 metres above the present lake level. The lake

LEGEND

Nonglacial

Alluvial fan, floodplain, deltaic deposits, organics, silt, sand and gravel.

Raised alluvial fan, floodplain, deltaic deposits, sand and gravel.

Glacial

Glaciolacustrine, varved clayey silt, terraces, Lake Penticton sediments.

Glaciofluvial, meltwater channels, terraces, sand & gravel, eskers, kames, knob and kettle topography.

Moraine, sandy silty till, bouldery, some gravel, hummocky to rolling, kettles.

Rock

Rock hills, benches and slopes, with patchy veneer of moraine.

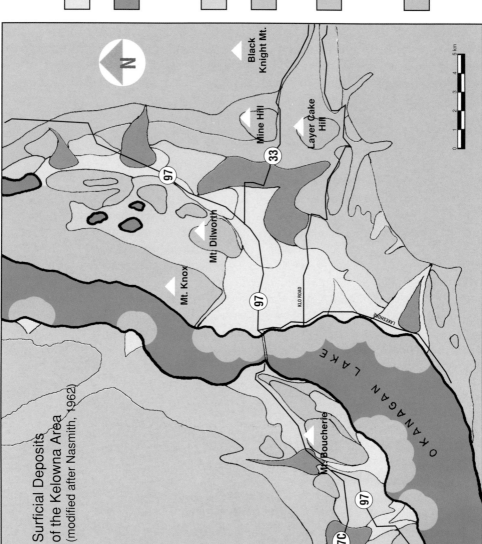

Surficial Deposits of the Kelowna Area
(modified after Nasmith, 1962)

Figure 13

46

extended as far north as Enderby, almost joining a similar lake in the Thompson River valley, and completely submerging the present sites of Penticton, Kelowna, Vernon and Armstrong.

The Okanagan glacier that last occupied the valley persisted for some time, melting very slowly as the water in Lake Penticton built up. Finally, as the core of stagnant ice melted, and as the ice dam periodically was breached, the level of the glacial lake began to drop. A series of terraces (silt bluffs) and erosional scarps up and down the valley were formed as the lake drained in distinct inter- vals. The last bit of glacial ice persisted so long in the valley that when it did finally melt, a depression was left that filled with water and formed the present Okanagan Lake. Thus, Okanagan Lake originated partly as a "kettle lake". A kettle is a depression in the ground where part of a glacier became buried. When the ice melts, the ground collapses and forms the depression called a kettle, or pit. If the kettle contains water, it is referred to as a kettle lake.

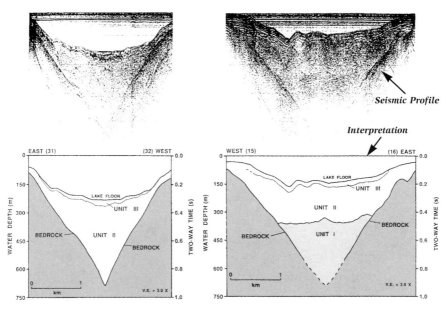

Figure 14: Profiles through Okanagan Lake from seismic studies
(from Eyles et al, 1990)

THE BURIED OKANAGAN VALLEY

It was not until long after the Plateau Volcanic event during Miocene-Pliocene time that the ancestral drainage of the present Okanagan landscape began to form. Due to structural weakness along parts of the Okanagan fault zone, the Okanagan Valley became a major stream valley, tributary to a large river system that drained south into the United States. By the time the climate had cooled near the end of the Tertiary Period, the region was still an upland which was slowly becoming dissected by the new "preglacial" river system. Most of the major valleys in the interior likely originate from this time and may have been interconnected.

During some of the glacial build-ups, ice over three kilometres thick accumulated above the deepest valleys. Ice this thick has tremendous scouring power

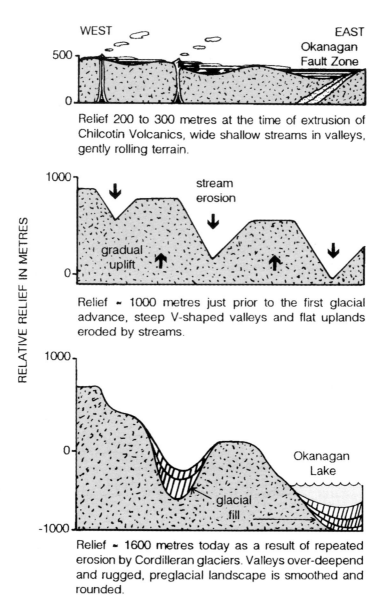

Relief 200 to 300 metres at the time of extrusion of Chilcotin Volcanics, wide shallow streams in valleys, gently rolling terrain.

Relief ~ 1000 metres just prior to the first glacial advance, steep V-shaped valleys and flat uplands eroded by streams.

Relief ~ 1600 metres today as a result of repeated erosion by Cordilleran glaciers. Valleys over-deepend and rugged, preglacial landscape is smoothed and rounded.

Figure 15: These diagrams illustrate uplift of the land and resulting erosion from a combination of stream and glacial activity in the last several million years in the Okanagan Valley.

near its base and sides. This explains the astounding overdeepening that affected the Okanagan Valley. The bedrock below Okanagan Lake is as much as 640 metres below sea level! The surface of the lake is 342 metres above sea level.

Our knowledge of features below the lake was enhanced by a seismic reflection survey conducted in October of 1989 (Eyles *et al*, 1990). A sample of profiles obtained in this work are shown in Figure 14. Of particular interest is the distinct and dramatic V-shape of the bedrock valley. It is apparent also that up to 750 metres of material has accumulated in the bedrock valley of the lake. Some of this is glacial and glaciolacustrine in origin, and some is related to sedimentation by streams that now empty into the lake.

The overall relief on the bedrock surface in today's landscape at Kelowna is 2810 metres (the difference in elevation between the deepest bedrock at the bottom of the lake, -640 metres, and that of neighbouring Little White Mountain, 2170 metres). This exceeds the relief of the Grand Canyon in Arizona at 1600 metres.

The onslaught of massive build-ups of glacial ice was destined to substantially modify the preglacial landforms and drainage systems. Overall the terrain had a similar distribution of high and low places (similar topography) in preglacial time as it has today. Major drainage systems and higher parts of the terrain had been already established. A summary of the accumulative uplift and erosion is illustrated in Figure 15.

OKANAGAN LAKE TODAY

Okanagan Lake is approximately 120 kilometres long and averages 3.5 kilometres wide. Its deepest point is 232 metres off Whiskey Island five kilometres north of Okanagan Centre. The bottom of the lake basin contains up to 750 metres of glacial material and nonglacial silt, sand and gravel, and thus the valley is partially buried.

The deep erosion along the Okanagan Valley occurred before the last glacial advance in the region as discussed previously and shown by the stratigraphic section near Okanagan Center (Figure 12). Earlier glaciers and interglacial streams must have been the main agents for deepening and gouging out the original valley. The lake has been therefore referred to as a fiord lake (Nasmith, 1962), resembling the spectacular fiords in Norway. The deepest fiord lake in British Columbia is Quesnel Lake, 500 kilometres north of Kelowna in the Cariboo Mountains; the water there is 530 metres in depth.

Okanagan Lake (Plate 9) has had a long and complicated prehistorical development. Factors influencing its origin include: rupture along the Okanagan fault over 50 million years ago; Tertiary volcanic and sedimentary activity; regional tectonic forces and stream dissection of an ancient upland; deep erosion from repeated glaciations, and the stagnation and melting of the Fraser Glacier that last occupied the valley 10,000 years ago.

The lake survives today because uplift has subsided. Base level is now controlled by the groundwater table in the region. The groundwater table is in turn

controlled by precipita-
tion that results in runoff

*Plate 9: Okanagan Lake
valley looking north from
the Knox Mountain
viewpoint (photo by John
D. Greenough). The ripple
in the centre distance
could be caused by
emergence of Ogopogo.*

by streams and seepage that becomes groundwater and moves through cracks and fissures in the highland rocks, flowing eventually to the lake. Finally, man has established controls with dams at Penticton and Okanagan Falls.

PRESENT DAY KELOWNA

The landscape and main geologic materials as it exists today is shown in a cross-section of the geology of the valley in Figure 8. It represents what you would find if the valley was cut open from near Mount Boucherie on the west, through the lake and subsurface, to below Little White Mountain in the east.

On the west is a fine example of a remnant upland (Hayman Upland) of the Thompson Plateau, capped with Plateau basalt at Carrot Mountain in the west. Proceeding east towards the lake, the cross-section shows the subsurface extent and volcanic fill of the Kelowna Caldera Basin. Note the deep conduits extending far below the volcanic neck of Mount Boucherie and the faults affecting the sub-surface. The Coryell intrusion which outcrops in Trepanier Creek and along the Highway 97C Connector represents the magma chamber that fed the extinct Tertiary volcanoes. Sandstones and conglomerates of the White Lake Formation can be seen covering the pre-existing rugged topography of the rift-like valley. Lake Okanagan shows a thick infilling of glacial and post-glacial sediments, and deep fiord-like erosion of its bedrock base. East of the lake is the metamorphic Shuswap complex and the bounding Okanagan fault zone. Arrows indicate the direction of former movement along the fault. Further to the east Little White Mountain is underlain by granitic intrusive rocks of the Jurassic-Cretaceous age Okanagan Batholith, with remnants of the intruded Monashee Gneiss.

CHAPTER 6

CLIMATIC CHANGE, THE LAST TEN THOUSAND YEARS AT KELOWNA

The glacial maximum during the last ice age occurred approximately 15,000 years ago after which global warming began. It took about five thousand years to finally melt the Fraser Glacier. During this time stagnant ice in the valleys cooled overlying air while air at the end of the glacier was heated through contact with mud, sand and gravel that absorbed the sun's rays. The cool dense air rushed down the glacier replacing the warm air and creating catabatic winds that extensively eroded the barren landscape composed of unconsolidated glacial sediments. Most large valleys during late stages of glacial retreat were likely plagued with daily sand storms as evidenced by extensive blankets of loess (silt sized particles) and sand on outwash terraces in the Kelowna area.

Disappearance of Ice

Ice melted fast off the highlands adjacent to Kelowna, but as the ice reached an elevation of approximately 900 metres, a still-stand seems to have occurred. That is, the glacier stopped melting and perhaps advanced for a certain period, probably in response to a temporary cooling. A gradient or slope of 20 metres per kilometre of the glacier surface up Mission Creek valley at this time can be approximated by connecting the elevations of the narrow parts of the valleys of Bellevue, KLO and Hydraulic Creeks. This means that the deeply eroded canyons (Myra Canyon, for example) of these creeks at higher elevations may have formed as a result of powerful rushes of meltwater coming off the highlands during initial melting of Fraser ice probably between 12,000 to 14,000 years ago. Much of the eroded material in this water was likely deposited on the surface of the stagnant glacier occupying the lower portion of the valley. Meanwhile, on the bare upland ancestors of the modern forest began to take root.

After the Ice Melted

By 10,000 years ago glacier ice had largely disappeared and Lake Penticton occupied the valley for less than a thousand years. Due to removal of the great weight of ice, the land began to rebound. This was accompanied by drainage of Lake Penticton, and this event is considered the beginning of the Holocene or recent Period. Geologists have a general idea of the climatic changes that occurred at Kelowna during the Holocene through studies of the Kelowna bog (number 22, Figure 19) just south of the airport (Alley, 1976) and from studies of cirque glaciers and deposits in higher parts of the province. The important agricultural soils in the Okanagan Valley formed also in this time interval.

Holocene glacial advances referred to as Neoglacial events (Ryder and Thompson, 1986) roughly correlate with climatic fluctuations inferred from the bog data as shown in Figure 16.

Vegetation changes have been determined by identifying spores and pollen preserved in a 2.75 metre thick drill core obtained from the bog and similar deposits across the province. Times of deposition of various layers in the bog were estimated by using two volcanic ash horizons of known age and radiocarbon dating of wood fragments found in the core.

Radiocarbon dating indicates that peat and organic clay at the bottom of the bog began accumulating on a lake bed approximately 8,500 years ago. The lake was probably a remnant of glacial Lake Penticton, largely drained during the preceding 500 years. Much of Kelowna was still under shallow water representing an extensive marshy delta, while the rest of the world was just emerging from the Stone Age.

Early Neoglacial/Holocene

Organic clay accumulated slowly in the Kelowna bog, reflecting the low nutrient content of the bare mineral glacial soils of the lake basin, or, possibly, the advance of early Holocene alpine glaciers representing a short but very cool moist interval. During this time, sparse vegetation had become established in the uplands. The dominant trees were Lodgepole Pine with some spruce and hemlock indicating cooler and moister conditions than present. High rainfall created many now-abandoned gullies and alluvial fans formed rapidly where major streams reached the valley floor. The Kelowna Bog was inundated periodically by floods associated with the Scotty Creek fan.

Hypsithermal/Middle Holocene

Arid conditions encouraging the growth of sagebrush and grass began approximately 7,000 years ago. This period during the Holocene lasted until about 4,000 years ago and is known as the Hypsithermal Interval. It is recognized over a broad region of North America. In the Okanagan, it is characterized on the surface by extensive wind blown sand blankets and dunes, and, in the forest by

Ponderosa Pine which reached its maximum 5,000 years ago. Minor glacial advances in alpine regions occurred 4,000 and 6,000 years ago in response to two short periods of cooling.

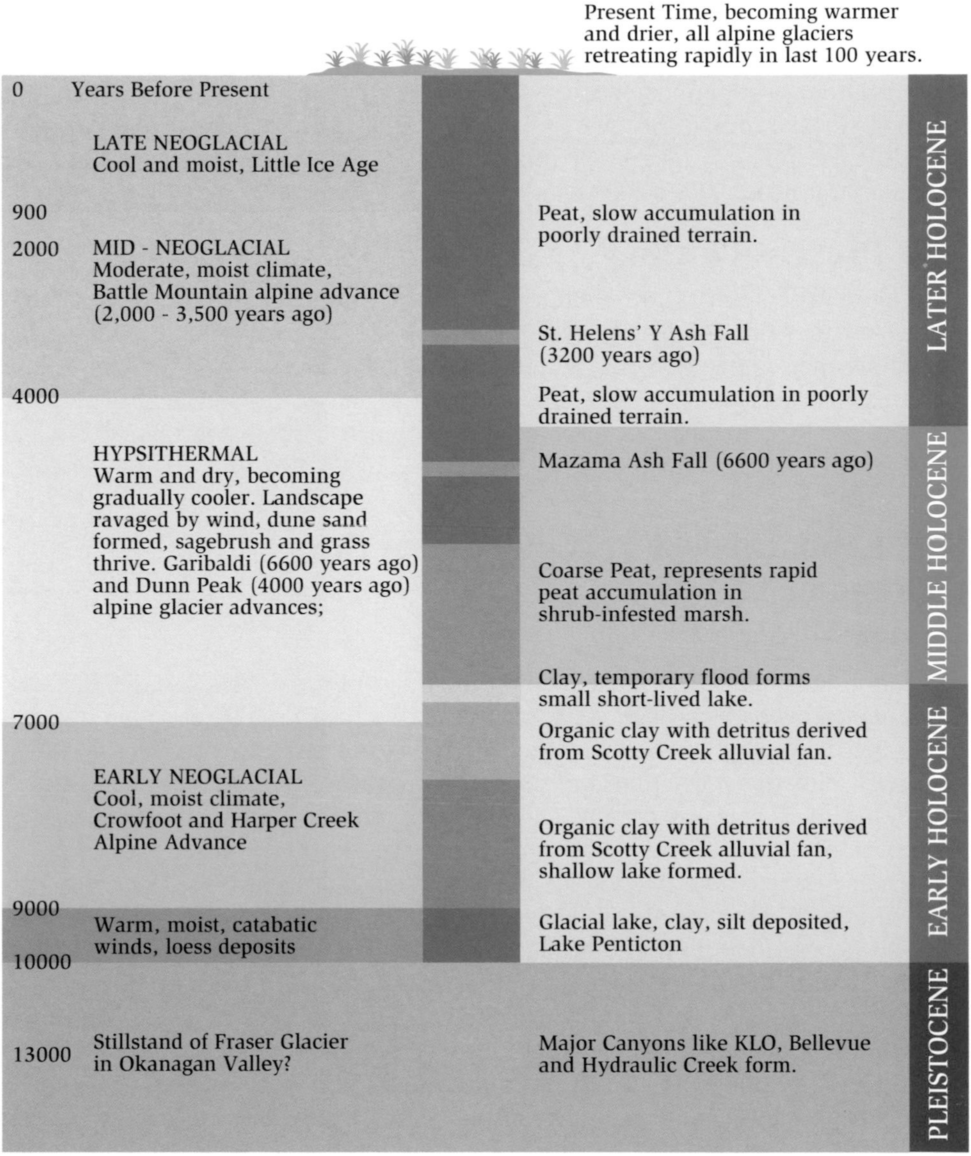

Present Time, becoming warmer and drier, all alpine glaciers retreating rapidly in last 100 years.

Years Before Present			
0			
	LATE NEOGLACIAL Cool and moist, Little Ice Age		LATER HOLOCENE
900		Peat, slow accumulation in poorly drained terrain.	
2000	MID - NEOGLACIAL Moderate, moist climate, Battle Mountain alpine advance (2,000 - 3,500 years ago)		
		St. Helens' Y Ash Fall (3200 years ago)	
4000		Peat, slow accumulation in poorly drained terrain.	
	HYPSITHERMAL Warm and dry, becoming gradually cooler. Landscape ravaged by wind, dune sand formed, sagebrush and grass thrive. Garibaldi (6600 years ago) and Dunn Peak (4000 years ago) alpine glacier advances;	Mazama Ash Fall (6600 years ago)	MIDDLE HOLOCENE
		Coarse Peat, represents rapid peat accumulation in shrub-infested marsh.	
		Clay, temporary flood forms small short-lived lake.	
7000		Organic clay with detritus derived from Scotty Creek alluvial fan.	EARLY HOLOCENE
	EARLY NEOGLACIAL Cool, moist climate, Crowfoot and Harper Creek Alpine Advance	Organic clay with detritus derived from Scotty Creek alluvial fan, shallow lake formed.	
9000	Warm, moist, catabatic winds, loess deposits	Glacial lake, clay, silt deposited, Lake Penticton	
10000			
13000	Stillstand of Fraser Glacier in Okanagan Valley?	Major Canyons like KLO, Bellevue and Hydraulic Creek form.	PLEISTOCENE

Figure 16: Geologic column through the Kelowna Bog showing inferred Holocene climatic fluctuations in the Okanagan Valley and Neoglacial events in alpine regions (modified respectively from Alley, 1976, and Ryder and Thompson, 1986). Location of the bog is given in Figure 19.

Mid-Neoglacial to Late Neoglacial/Late Holocene

During the next two thousand years the climate moderated, moist conditions returned and more exuberant vegetative growth stabilized most sand dunes. In alpine areas a Late Holocene cirque glacial advance occurred 3,500 to 2,000 years ago and was quite extensive.

Locally, the last four thousand years in the Okanagan are characterized by three cool and wet periods versus warm and dry climate fluctuations. Birch and aspen flourished during the two cool periods. The latest of these correlates with the Little Ice Age advance of alpine glaciers in the Pacific Northwest and the Canadian Cordillera 900 to 100 years ago.

The Present Century

The climate appears to be entering a warm and dry phase; however, recent studies of cores through glacial ice and detailed dating of ice in the Greenland Ice Cap show that climatic swings within the Holocene are far more dynamic than previously suspected. What this all means is that neither the intensity of climatic changes nor their frequency can be predicted, which is some consolation to local weather forecasters.

Soil Landscapes & Agriculture of the Okanagan Valley

by Herb A. Luttmerding

Soil in the pedological sense refers to that part of the earth's surface that supports plant growth. It consists of a zone at the surface usually less than a metre thick. Soil is formed by the interaction of soil parent material (surficial geologic deposits), climate, vegetation and landscape position (moisture conditions), all integrated over time. In the Okanagan Valley, all soil parent materials are of glacial or post-glacial origin and age. Thus, the last ten thousand years is an important geologic time interval for soil formation and has resulted in the development of a broad range of soil landscapes (Figure 17).

The general distribution and characteristics of Okanagan soils are given in Figure 17. In the south Okanagan area, between Penticton and the U.S.A. border, the valley bottom soils are mainly developed in sandy and gravelly, coarse textured glaciofluvial and alluvial deposits that are well or rapidly drained and developed under grassland vegetation. These are mainly Orthic Dark Brown or Orthic Brown Chernozem soils. Where topography is suitable, these soils support heat-loving tree fruits, vegetables and grapes, all produced under irrigation. The alluvial floodplain of the Okanagan River has sandy to silty, imperfectly to poorly drained soils, often strongly calcareous; they have Regosolic or Gleysoic soil development.

South Okanagan valley slopes mainly have moderately coarse textured, well drained soils developed in morainal or colluvial materials, commonly interspersed with bedrock outcrops. Soil development ranges from Orthic Dark Brown or Orthic Black Chernozems in grassland areas to Eutric Brunisols under forest. Land use is mainly cattle grazing and forest production. The valley slopes are also important wildlife areas, particularly during the winter.

Further north, between Penticton and Summerland, coarse textured soils of glaciofluvial and fluvial origin with Orthic Dark Brown or Eutric Brunisol soil development are prevalent. In the Summerland area particularly, fine sandy to silty eolian cappings overlie the gravels and sands. Another notable feature of the Summerland-Penticton-Naramata area is the silty glaciolacustrine terraces (glacial Lake Penticton) flanking Okanagan Lake. The soils on these deposits are mostly Brown Chernozems, strongly gullied and susceptible to piping (Figure 27). The subsoils are also strongly calcareous. Irrigated tree fruits are the usual crops in this area.

The valley widens to several kilometres in the Westbank - Kelowna - Winfield area. Coarse textured, rapidly drained soils are still common although other soils prevail as well. Silty to clayey, well or moderately well drained soils of glaciolacustrine origin are common in the Westbank area and in the Glenmore Valley. Soil development here is dominantly Gray Luvisol with some Orthic Dark Brown Chernozems. Moderately textured, Eutric Brunisol or Gray Luvisol soils of morainal origin are also common, particularly along the valley sides. The fluvial delta/fan of Mission Creek occupies a large area on the east side of Okanagan Lake in the vicinity of Kelowna. A water table is usually present at various depths and soil development of these sandy to silty, moderately to poorly drained soils ranges from Gleyed Regosols to various Gleysols. A few small organic areas are also present. Agricultural use of the soils in the Westbank - Kelowna - Winfield area is mainly for tree fruits and grapes although some forage crops and vegetables are also produced. Irrigation is usual. The area is also subject to strong urbanization pressures.

In the Vernon - Armstrong area, much of the valley bottom is dominated by soils developed in clayey glaciolacustrine sediments. Well drained, moderately pervious Gray Luvisol soils (also some Solonetzic soils) are common and mostly used for non-irrigated forage and small grain production. Sandy and gravelly fluvial and glaciofluvial soils predominate on Grandview Flats and in parts of the Coldstream Valley. These well and rapidly drained soils have thick surface layers enriched with organic matter, classified as Orthic Black Chernozems. Agricultural production on these soils, essentially all irrigated, ranges from forage and silage corn to tree fruits and small fruits and vegetables. Most of the higher locations in the valley consist of medium or moderately coarse textured soils developed in morainal material. These soils are well drained sometimes stony Gray Luvisols or Eutric Brunisols.

The Okanagan Valley is deeply incised into the Thompson Plateau by at least 1,000 metres. Slopes on the flank of this upland north from Penticton are mainly forested except for some south facing parts of tributary valleys that are grass and

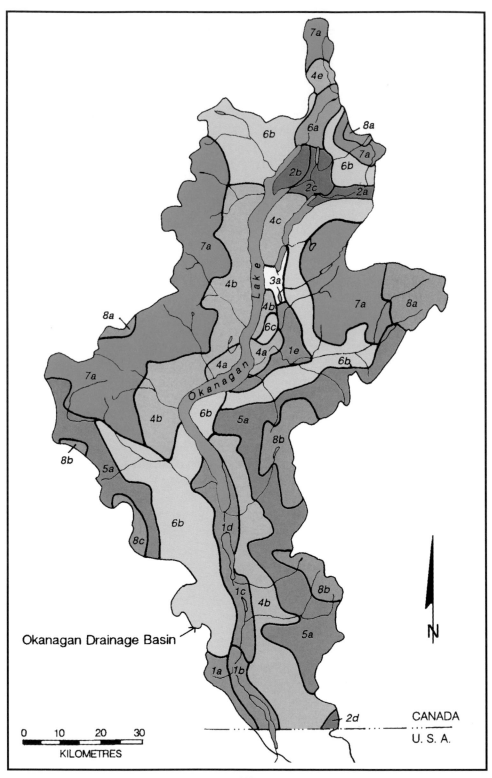

Okanagan Drainage Basin

KILOMETRES
0   10   20   30

N

CANADA
U. S. A.

Figure 17 (opposite page): Soil landscapes of the Okanagan watershed (modified after Agriculture Canada, 1993).

FIGURE 17 – LEGEND

SOIL LANDSCAPES OF THE OKANAGAN WATERSHED

1. DOMINANTLY DARK BROWN CHERNOZEM SOILS
   1A   Morainal, inclusions of Brown soils and Eutric Brunisol colluvial soils.
   1B   Glaciofluvial and alluvial, inclusions of Brown Soils.
   1C   Glaciofluvial, inclusions of Regosolic alluvium.
   1D   Glaciofluvial, substantial inclusions of silty Brown lacustrine soils.
   1E   Glaciofluvial and morainal soils.

2. DOMINANTLY BLACK CHERNOZEM SOILS
   2A   Alluvial, inclusions of Gleysolic soils.
   2B   Morainal, inclusions of lithic colluvial soils.
   2C   Morainal, substantial inclusions of clayey Dark Gray lacustrine soils.
   2D   Loamy morainal, inclusions of lithic Eutric Brunisol colluvial soils.

3 DOMINANTLY DARK GRAY CHERNOZEM SOILS
   3A   Glaciofluvial, inclusions of moderately coarse Dark Brown morainal soils.

4. DOMINANTLY EUTRIC BRUNISOL SOILS
   4A   Morainal, inclusions of clayey Gray Luvisol lacustrine soils.
   4B   Colluvial, inclusions of loamy Gray Luvisol morainal soils and rock outcrop.
   4C   Colluvial, inclusions of loamy Black morainal soils and rock outcrop.
   4D   Lithic colluvial, substantial inclusions of rock outcrop.
   4E   Morainal, inclusions of coarse Black glaciofluvial soils.

5. DOMINANTLY DYSTRIC BRUNISOL SOILS
   5A   Morainal, inclusions of coarse lithic colluvial soils.

6. DOMINANTLY GRAY LUVISOL SOILS
   6A   Lacustrine, clayey, inclusions of coarse glaciofluvial Eutric Brunisol soils.
   6B   Morainal, inclusions of moderately coarse lithic Eutric Brunisols soils.
   6C   Lacustrine, clayey, inclusions of Dark Brown and moderately coarse Eutric Brunisol colluvial soils.

7. DOMINANTLY BRUNISOLIC GRAY LUVISOL SOILS
   7A   Morainal, inclusions of moderately coarse lithic Dystric Brunisol colluvial soils.

8. DOMINANTLY HUMO-FERRIC PODZOL SOILS
   8A   Morainal, inclusions of lithic colluvial soils.
   8B   Morainal, inclusions of lithic colluvial soils.
   8C   Lithic colluvial, inclusions of loamy morainal soils.

9. DOMINANTLY GLEYSOLIC SOILS
   9A   Alluvial, poorly drained, substantial inclusions of coarse loamy imperfectly drained Regosolic soils.

shrub covered. The soils are moderately coarse textured, well drained and steep or moderately steep. They are developed in thin morainal material and colluvium, either over bedrock or interspersed with bedrock outcrops. Soil development consists dominantly of Eutric Brunisols with Black Chernozems in grassy areas.

The rolling forested plateau or upland flanking the Okanagan Valley is mantled with deposits of glacial moraine origin. The soils are generally moderately coarse textured, well or moderately well drained but include scattered, depressional, poorly drained organic areas. The usual soil development ranges from neutral Eutric Brunisols at lower elevations through Dystric Brunisols to strongly acid

Podzols at the highest elevations. Gray Luvisols also occur where the soil parent material is medium textured.

Climatically, the Okanagan Valley is driest and hottest in the south and gradually becomes somewhat cooler and moister in the north. Similar conditions also occur with increasing elevation from the valley floor to the upland region. Soil development reflects this climatic variability, with Dark Brown and Brown Chernozems dominating in the south and Dystric Brunisols or Podzols the usual development at upper elevations.

CHAPTER **7**

ANCIENT PEOPLES OF THE OKANAGAN

Controversy still exists about the dates and routes used by the first people of North America, much less the more specific questions of aboriginal settlers in the Okanagan. Reliable archeological evidence supports people settling in North America at least 20,000 years ago. Many of the sites that support this date are south of the Okanagan for the obvious reason that the land here was covered by ice until at least 15,000 years ago. However, there were people living south of the Okanagan in the Columbia River basin about 11,000 years ago, and at the Charlie Lake Cave site in northern British Columbia at least 10,700 years ago (Fladmark *et al*, 1988). It is presumed that it was the northward migration up the Columbia River basin, and, possibly, the Fraser River basin, that led to the peopling of the Okanagan some 9,000 years ago (Borden, 1979, Fladmark, 1983, Baker, 1990). So far exact dates of first settlement are unknown because very little systematic archeological work has been done in the Okanagan Valley area. It is plausible, however, that the higher elevations of the Okanagan Highland or the Thompson Plateau were visited first since there may have been a stillstand during the retreat of the Fraser Glacier about 13,000 years ago (see Chapter Five), by which time ice above an elevation of 900 metres may have melted.

The Okanagans

While there has been very little study of the earliest peoples of the Okanagan, we do know a little more about their likely descendants, the Okanagan people of 3,000 to 5,000 years ago. At the height of Okanagan culture, at least 3,000 years ago, it is estimated some 12,000 people lived in this valley and the surrounding areas (Baker, 1990). Linguistic and ethnographic data suggest that traditional Okanagan territory included the Okanagan Valley as well as the Arrow and Slocan Lakes (Figure 18). In addition, areas populated south of the 49th parallel included the Okanogan River south to Brewster, Kettle Falls and the Colville River (Turner *et al*,

1980; Baker, 1990). Within this approximately 72,000 square kilometres of territory, some seven dialects of the Okanagan language were spoken (Turner *et al*, 1980).

The Okanagan language is part of the Interior Salish language division of the Salishan language family. As Baker suggests these peoples were largely centred around the Okanagan valley itself and may be considered typical of Okanagan culture.

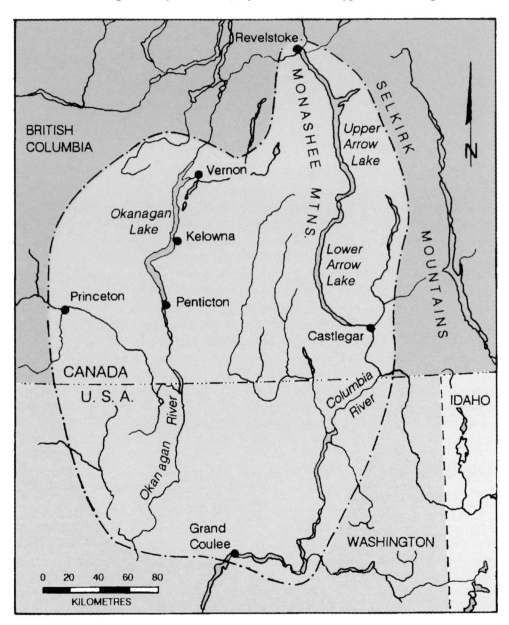

Figure 18: Traditional Okanagan Territory.

Okanagan Plateau Pithouse Tradition

Most of the limited archeological research about the Okanagans has centred around 4,000 to 200 years before present. Richards and Rousseau (1987) have presented a synthesis of the various research and frameworks proposed for this time period. They have called the period from approximately 4,000 to 200 years before present the "Plateau Pithouse Tradition". One of the central distinguishing characteristics of life in this period is the pithouse or "kekuli".

Okanagan Way of Life

The Okanagan people of this time lived a rich life, moving between traditional areas throughout the year to fish, hunt or collect food, depending on the season. In this sense, they may be called hunter-gatherers. In the winter months they lived in villages of ecologically efficient pithouses. These semi-round structures, accommodating 6 to 10 extended family members, were made by digging out a circular or rectangular area of the earth to a depth of about one metre and then using four main poles as roof supports. The roof was covered with smaller branches and earth making an exceptionally warm and heat efficient dwelling for the cold winter months. There was a squarish opening at the top created by the four main roof rafters. Often there was a side entrance to the pithouse. Villages might contain anywhere from four to over one hundred such dwellings. Each village was largely autonomous with its own headman or chief, depending on size (Hudson, 1990). Many of the village sites of this early settlement have been destroyed by development in the Okanagan Valley. Protected areas such as Okanagan Mountain Park still contain relatively undisturbed sites. While large collections of pithouses have not been examined in the Okanagan, in the Kamloops area a collection of more than 200 pithouses has been recorded (Wilson and Carlson, 1980). Over time there were changes in pithouse design, possibly reflecting climatic changes. In addition to the pithouses there were also smaller pits used to store foods as well as pits to roast foods such as bitterroot. An example of a pithouse is on display at the Kelowna Museum.

Food Gathering

In the Spring the extended family groups would move from the winter village to their spring sites which would involve a more mobile form of dwelling, possibly woven tule mat structures. These structures may have had a rectangular floor plan with an inverted "V" roof covered with woven tule mats (Turner et al, 1980). Since the horse was not introduced into the Okanagan until after 1730 (Keyser, 1992), dogs harnessed to travois would be used to help transport goods. Early spring plants such as Bitterroot (Lewisia rediviva), "Spitlem" in Okanagan language, would be harvested and processed in large rock roasting pits according to traditional methods. Some roasting pits scattered throughout the Okanagan remain today, an example of which can be seen in Okanagan Mountain Park. In addition to Bitterroot, other plants such as Balsam root would be harvested along with year round staples such as fish and game.

Fishing

Fish were a major food resource for the Okanagans. Although all varieties of fish were utilized - trout, kokanee, coarse fish, sockeye and chinook salmon - it was the salmon that formed the most important species. As with all food gathering activities there was an associated pattern and ritual which served to both conserve and distribute the resource equitably. There was a "Salmon Chief" who not only directed the construction of the wiers and traps but also controlled the distribution of the catch. Salmon fishing could be significant social occasions. Since all members of the family could be involved in the fishing and processing, this activity might stretch over some weeks in the early Fall. This would be a good opportunity for families to come together, and marriages might be arranged at such times (Hudson, 1990). The major salmon fishing site in Okanagan territory was Okanagan Falls. Other sites available to the Okanagans were Kettle Falls and areas in Shuswap territory. The Okanagans may have also traded for salmon from sites not in their traditional territory. Both Okanagan and Kettle Falls localities were greatly affected by the reservoir of Grand Coulee Dam, but these sites still present the best prospects for additional archeologic discoveries.

Hunting

There were usually four major hunting expeditions during the year - the mid winter, spring, fall and early winter hunts. This could vary of course depending on need. Hunters could be away as long as one to two months, and distance traveled could be large. In the fall, the hunters would travel to the Okanagan Highlands in search of game. At least one Okanagan Highland site has been recorded.

Large game included bear, elk (possibly Roosevelt), deer (both White Tail and Mule), moose, mountain goat and sheep. Smaller game included rabbit, beaver, grouse, duck, martin, turtle, squirrel and others. As with fishing there was usually a hunt leader and a ritual preceded all the major hunts, which were group activities (Baker, 1990). The fall hunt would concentrate on bear, elk, moose and deer while the late winter was mainly for sheep. In the mid-winter the hunt would concentrate on deer, especially if the snow was crusted enough to support the hunters, but not the deer. Smaller game were hunted all year and formed an important part of the food resource. There are several pictograph panels that record hunting activities (Corner, 1968).

Social Organization and Activities

The Okanagan way of life involved many group activities but preserved a high degree of family and personal autonomy. Winter villages could be occupied by a few or many families. Main winter villages would have a single chief. Each large winter village would be considered a band. Membership within a village was fluid and families were free to move from one village to another (Hudson, 1990; Bailey and Rousseau, 1994). Positions such as the Salmon Chief and hunt leader were chosen on ability and spiritual powers. Interaction between villages often occurred at communal food gathering areas, especially during fishing season. There were also other social occasions that promoted festive gathering. On June 30th, 1877, the geologist George Dawson while on a trip along the old aboriginal trail near Naramata noted a large group of Okanagans on their way home from a "great potlatch" held at the head of the lake [Vernon area] (Cole and Lockner, 1989). This socialization was likely a historic custom. It provided an opportunity for the Okanagan people living at the foot of the lake [now Penticton] to socialize and trade with other Okanagans from the head of the lake.

Pictographs, Reflections and Potential

If as Baker (1990) suggests there were 12,000 people living in the larger Okanagan territory, then Okanagan life must have been rich and vibrant. Further evidence for this is recorded in the many pictographs throughout Okanagan territory. Pictograph themes vary from spiritual visions to hunting practices (Plate 10).

Plate 10: A pictograph on a steep rock cliff in Okanagan Mountain Park displays man and animals. There are numerous pictograph sites in the Okanagan Valley region but no systematic and scientific inventories have been done. Photo by George Ewonus.

While direct precision dating of the pictographs has not yet been attempted there is archeological evidence suggesting that some pictographs are at least 2,000 years old (Copp, 1980). A pictograph spall on the adjacent Columbia plateau at Good Creek has been archeologically dated to between 6,000 and 7,000 years ago

(Keyser, 1992). Furthermore, an inventory of pictographs has never been attempted and although many have been discovered their locations are closely guarded secrets to protect against vandalism.

Often a pictograph panel may tell something about an adjacent village site. In the case of the Good Creek winter village, which may have also been a food processing site, a nearby pictograph panel depicts hunting activities (Bailey and Rousseau, 1994). Throughout the Okanagan valley many beaches and bays still show evidence of ancient Okanagan people's use.

Role of Geology

Earth Science has a direct role in assisting archaeologists. Firstly, terrain scientists are capable of identifying past terrestrial environments that may have controlled the early migration of the Okanagan people. The most obvious example is the stranded shoreline of glacial Lake Penticton. This shoreline occurs at an elevation of between 500 and 525 metres and would have been a natural corridor to follow. In places there is a well developed sand beach in former embayments along the rock slopes of the valley. These are prime archeologic sites for early habitation (see Chapter Eight). Geologists may also be able to pin-point former streams that entered the lake, which may have been particularly attractive to early people due to fishing potential. Even the location of warm or cold groundwater springs, especially in upland regions, may provide a starting point for future discoveries. Close observation of air photographs may reveal fracture zones and cliffs in the bedrock which could be ideal sites for pictographs.

When a site is discovered, details regarding the origin of the sediments deposited at the site as revealed by geologic study can be of great benefit in the interpretation of climatic conditions during the site's occupation.

Geologists and archaeologists also complement each other's work by accumulating data that provide more precise chronologies of post-glacial historic events. This assists the archaeologists in tracing the evolution of successive cultures and allows them to correlate to other more distant sequences of habitation. An example of this is the summary of the last ten thousand years presented in Chapter Six. It is now possible to include an archeologic history which along with the other data begins to present a more comprehensive view of this time period.

Future Potential

Approximately 350 archeologic sites are now known to exist in the vicinity of Okanagan Lake. It is estimated that the Okanagan could have over 1,000 archeologic sites, and there have been virtually no upland site discoveries. Despite this, our understanding of the ancient peoples of the Okanagan is extremely limited. Collections of artifacts and systematic site descriptions are very rare. The current rate of development in the Okanagan Valley underscores the importance and need for further geological, ethnographic and archeological research, and offers students an exciting career alternative.

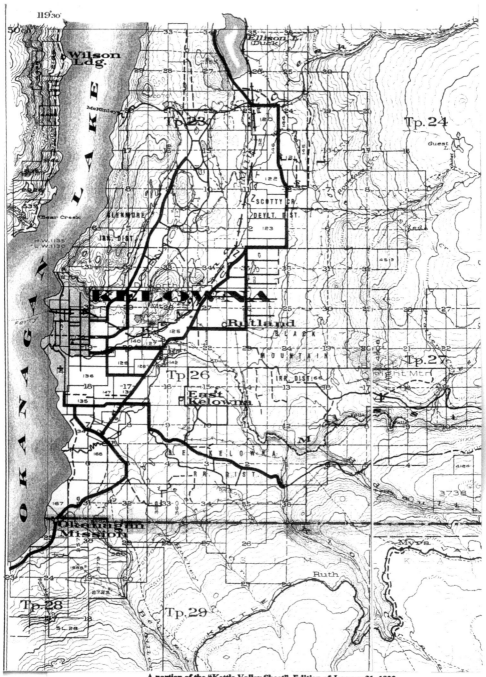

A portion of the "Kettle Valley Sheet", Edition of January 31, 1923.
This map was surveyed by J.D.McCaw for Department of Lands,
British Columbia. It is a topographic map at a scale of one inch = two miles.

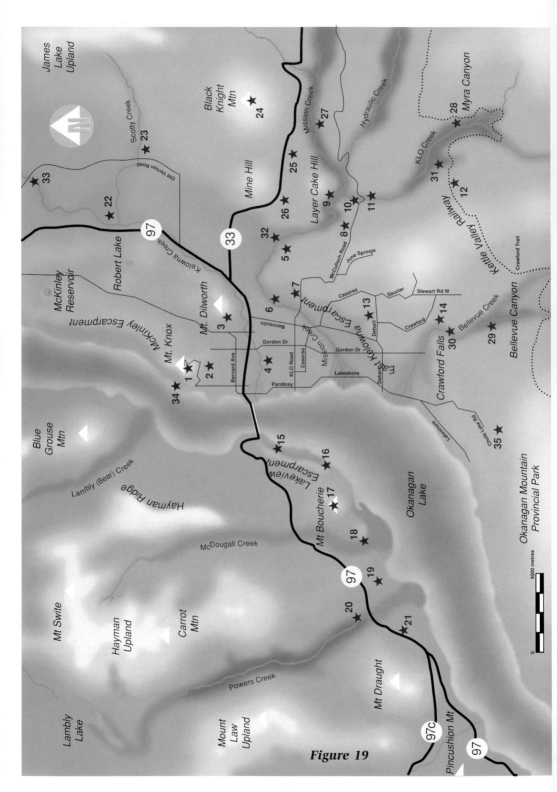

Figure 19

CHAPTER 8

GEOLOGIC LANDMARKS OF THE KELOWNA AREA

Specific geological features that are local scenic landmarks in the Kelowna area are described in this Chapter which is intended to be used in conjunction with a self-guided tour called *"A Sight-seer's Delight"* in Appendix A. The features are numbered and shown along with main roads on the map of Figure 19.

Figure 19 (opposite page): Location map of Geologic Landmark Features in the Kelowna area. Bracketed numbers in text refer to numbers on the map, keyed to an accompanying list of the features. Note that a few of the features listed are not discussed in the text.

LIST OF GEOLOGIC LANDMARKS IN FIGURE 19

1 Knox Mountain Viewpoint
2 Varved Silt Terraces, Glacial Lake Penticton
3 Mount Dilworth Escarpment
4 Flatlands of Kelowna and Rutland
5 Terraces of Rutland and the Rutland Fan
6 Mission Creek Regional Park
7 Varved Clay, Glacial Lake Penticton
8 Hummocky Moraine
9 Gallagher's Canyon
10 Till Outcrops
11 Quarry, Shuswap Rocks
12 Kettle Valley Railway, Plateau Basalt
13 East Kelowna Fan
14 Beach Deposit, Glacial Lake Penticton
15 Lambly Creek Basalt Cliff, Lakeview
16 Kalamoir Regional Park
17 Mount Boucherie Columns
18 Sandstone Cavities, McDougall Creek Fan

19 Varved Clay, Boucherie and Gellatly Roads
20 Glen Canyon Regional Park
21 Coal Beds, Fossil Trees
22 Kelowna Bog
23 Lateral Moraine
24 Roche Moutonnée
25 Eskers and Kames
26 Kettle Lake, Garner and Belgo Ponds
27 Mission Creek Waterfall
28 Myra Canyon
29 Bellevue Canyon
30 Crawford Falls
31 Warm Spring
32 Cutbank of Mission Creek, Rutland Fan
33 Mill (Kelowna) Creek Falls
34 Paul's Tomb
35 Kelowna Crags

Knox Mountain Viewpoint (1)

From the observation station about a three minute walk from the parking lot at the top of Knox Mountain Park (Figure 19) many of the geologic features discussed in this and previous chapters can be observed in one spectacular panoramic view. Points of interest are shown in a directional rosette in Figure 20.

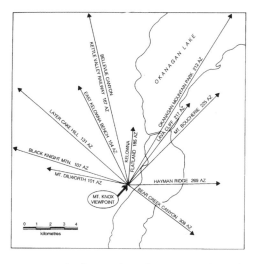

Figure 20: Directional rosette for Knox Mountain viewpoint, southern aspect (imagine standing at the kiosk and looking south). Arrows indicate the direction in degrees Azimuth. For example, 180 AZ would be due South.

To the southeast, in the distance, the slanting rock slabs of the Precambrian Shuswap metamorphic rocks outcrop along the east side of Okanagan Lake. On the west side are hills in the Westbank area composed of volcanic and sedimentary rocks of the Tertiary Period (Eocene Epoch, 37 to 58 million years ago). Separating the two is the Okanagan fault zone which runs through East Kelowna and the Mission and then toward Vernon. One can appreciate the amount of

Plate 10a: A view to the south from Knox Mountain viewpoint shows dipping metamorphic strata in the distant Okanagan Mountain Park and a volcanic dome, Mount Boucherie, looming at the right. Photo by John D. Greenough.

vertical displacement on the Okanagan fault since the Tertiary time by noting that when the volcanic rocks were forming at the surface of the earth, the Shuswap rocks were buried several kilometres down in the earth!

During the Tertiary a wide rugged valley (graben) existed with perhaps some rudimentary similarities to the present valley. However, you are now standing in what was part of a large caldera (volcanic) complex that stretched from south of Mount Boucherie to the northern edge of the city (close to the airport). The tan colored rocks underfoot at Knox Mountain represent andesite lava flows and ash deposits of the Eocene Marron Formation produced by the volcano. Late in the Tertiary there was a major river flowing through the valley.

Only 760,000 years ago another volcanic event affected the valley and produced the Lambly Creek basalt visible as cliffs above the floating bridge on the west side of the lake (Plate 6). These are the youngest rocks in the Kelowna area.

The last glaciation had a dramatic effect in shaping the landforms visible from Knox Mountain. Beginning at least 1.6 million years ago much of the present valley was carved out by repeated advances of ice sheets so thick (3 km) that the ice was higher than mountain tops visible in the distance! The bedrock base of Okanagan Lake lies almost one kilometre below your feet, acting as testament to the incredible grinding power of the ice sheet. Deep scratches (striae) etched into the rocks at the top of Knox Mountain (within 30 metres to the north of the lookout point) by boulders embedded in the base of the Fraser Glacier indicate the local direction of ice movement.

Plate 11: A northerly view of Knox and Dilworth Mountains from near the end of Mission Ridge Drive in Crawford Estates, level with the maximum height of glacial Lake Penticton. The flatland of Kelowna was under 100 metres of water 10,000 years ago. Grouse Mountain is the peak on the left. Glaciation has not entirely removed the resemblance of these mountains to the towering volcanoes they once were.

Glacial Lake Penticton Silt Terraces (2)

Nestled against Knox and Dilworth Mountains are remnants of the extensive lake that developed as the Fraser Glacier melted. Glacial Lake Penticton reached an elevation of about 460 metres or 1500 feet above sea level which is over 100 metres (370 feet) above the present level of Okanagan Lake.

Deposits formed in the glacial lake dominate the lower valley slopes forming bench-like landforms on both sides of Okanagan Valley and above the flatland of the main part of the City (Plates 10 and 11). The deposits consist mainly of silt with some sand and clay. They are known locally as silt bluffs, and adorn Highway 97 and the lake shore between Kelowna and Penticton. Bench levels can be correlated from one side of the valley to the other. Unfortunately, the picturesque silt bluffs of the Okanagan pose geological hazards as they occasionally fail, causing local landslides that can damage roads and buildings and be hazardous to life (see Chapter Nine).

Mount Dilworth Escarpment (3)

Plate 12: Feldspathic lava outcrops of the Marama Formation form this dramatic cliff bordering the fairway of the Kelowna Golf and Country Club. Glacial and ancient stream erosion combined to form this feature during the Pleistocene Period.

Feldspathic lava of the Marama Formation (Figure 5) is exposed in a steep cliff which borders the Kelowna Golf and Country Club. The cliff was gouged out mainly by glacial action. Talus at the base of the scarp is ideal habitat for a thriving population of marmots.

Plate 13: The volcanic rocks of Dilworth Mountain have been eroded by rainwater to form a series of hoodoos, visible from Knox Mountain viewpoint where this photo was taken.

Flatland of Kelowna and Rutland (4)

A series of catastrophic floods likely struck the Okanagan whenever glacial Lake Penticton suddenly drained. Perhaps up to 100 metres of the same material forming present day bluffs was locally removed from the valley sides. This likely occurred in a series of water releases as the ice dam at Okanagan Falls was periodically breached and as the land rose in response to the disappearance of ice that had depressed the rocks below. The floor of that former gigantic spillway is now occupied by the peaceful and unassuming communities of Rutland and Kelowna.

Sediments deposited on the former spillway are composed of alternating layers of silt, sand and gravel with some organic-bearing clay beds. These deposits represent deltaic and shallow water deposits and marshes from runoff of Mission and Mill (Kelowna) Creeks which were far larger streams seven to eight thousand years ago. The streams flowed into a shallow bay of an early stage of Okanagan Lake. The bay gradually infilled forming a lowland on which Kelowna and Rutland were built (see Surficial Geology map, Figure 13). Duck Lake and Ellison Lake were likely isolated from early Lake Okanagan by similar extensive alluvial fans deposited on the valley floor by early activity of streams such as Mill Creek and Scotty Creek.

Isolated knolls of sand and gravel on the northern Kelowna flatland represent the top beds of fan or deltaic deposits dissected when the last remnants of glacial Lake Penticton drained. The gravel is utilized as aggregate and the low sand ridges provide ideal foundation conditions for small buildings.

Southward, the flatlands are composed of silt, clay and fine sand that contains plant remains and organic material such as peat. This provides evidence for a prolonged period of marsh development along the delta front in the flatlands during post-glacial time. Prior to urbanization the flatland was marked by a number of ponds representing cutoff meanders and flood channels of the various creeks that flowed across the area. Naturalists have been struggling for years to preserve the few remaining remnants of these ponds.

Terraces of Rutland and the Rutland Fan (5)

Picturesque orchards blanket the terraces of the eastern part of Kelowna and Rutland. As Lake Penticton was filling due to melting of the Fraser Glacier about ten thousand years ago, major meltwater poured out of tributary valleys, the largest of which is Mission Creek valley. A huge outwash delta known as the Rutland Fan formed at the end of Mission Creek valley. As the delta grew out into the lake its sand and gravel covered clay sediments deposited earlier along the edge of the lake. These sand and gravel deposits now form the vegetable and fruit producing terraces of Rutland.

Mission Creek Regional Park (6)

Plate 14: A pillar of glacial till in Mission Creek Park overlooks the flatland of Kelowna. Dilworth Mountain is in the background.

Mission Creek Regional Park straddles present-day Mission Creek and a terrace composed partly of silt and clay deposited in Lake Penticton about 9000 years ago, massive till (Plate 14) and hummocky outwash sand and gravel, capped in places with eolian sand.

Pits or kettles in the hummocky outwash terrain in the southern part of the park resulted from deposition of sand and gravel from meltwater flowing around large stagnant blocks of ice left behind as the Fraser Glacier receded. In places the kettles are occupied by ponds that teem with aquatic life (turtles are children's favourites) and provide habitat for numerous water birds.

Mission Creek today supplies one third of the total runoff to Lake Okanagan, and is the main spawning channel of Kokanee. The land-locked salmon likely made their way into the Okanagan when a remnant of glacial Lake Penticton was connected by streams to the Pacific Ocean. (Note: Perhaps ancestors of Ogopogo also migrated at this time.)

Varved Clay, Glacial Lake Penticton (7)

Varved clay from glacial Lake Penticton occurs along the north side of KLO Road just past Mission Creek bridge (Figure 21 and Plate 15).

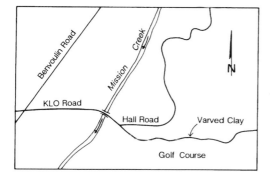

Figure 21

These rhythmic deposits are common in glacial lakes and better examples cannot be found anywhere. The thick light-colored layers were deposited in the summer when glacial streams carried an abundant supply of silt into the lake. Thin dark layers formed during the winter when stream freeze-up curtailed the silt supply. Thus, a year's deposition is represented by one light and one dark layer. How many years did it take this deposit exposed here to form? The outcrop on KLO Road also contains 2 to 4 cm long dropstones, rocks rafted out into the lake by icebergs and then dropped when the ice melted.

Plate 15: Varved clay and silt deposited in glacial Lake Penticton outcrops on KLO Road. (See Figure 21).

Hummocky Moraine, East Kelowna (8)

The area between June Springs Road and KLO Creek valley consists of hummocky moraine, an area of hills and depressions composed of sand and gravel, and till. These deposits formed about 10,000 years ago when a lobe of glacial ice occupying Mission Creek Valley stagnated. This caused till and glacial outwash sediments to accumulate at the end of the glacier. This material eventually blocked drainage from the Mission Creek valley forming a long narrow glacial lake up Mission Creek valley and Belgo Creek valley.

Depressions in the landscape along this part of McCulloch Road are called kettles and the hills are termed knobs, thus "knob and kettle" topography is characteristic of hummocky moraine. McCulloch Road is built partly on the edge of a meltwater channel from a high stage of KLO Creek that partly dissected the hummocky moraine.

Gallagher's Canyon & Scenic Canyon Regional Park (9)

Ancient high levels of Mission Creek have carved a deep and highly picturesque canyon, Gallagher's Canyon, that extends for seven kilometres upstream. Cataracts, falls, rapids and colorful rocks of the Shuswap Complex (Monashee Gneiss) and dramatic cliffs of Eocene volcanic rocks and glacial deposits combine to form this picturesque and rugged canyon. The main Mission Creek waterfall (Plate 16) is over 20 metres high and presents an impressive example of rock sculpturing that few people have seen.

Other geological focal points in the Gallagher's Canyon area include a 200 metre high wall of layered Tertiary volcanic rocks making up Layer Cake Hill, Pinnacle Rock (see photo on front of book), and excellent examples of folds and faults in sandstone bearing witness to the tremendous mountain building forces that have affected the Okanagan Valley.

Plate 16: The waterfall on Mission Creek near the city limit is over 20 metres high but it is difficult to access unless you are young like these daredevils. This torturous cataract is one of the most spectacular natural features in the Kelowna area.

The lower part of the canyon was the centre of an active gold mining camp in the late 1800's (see Chapter Eleven for more on gold and Dan Gallagher). Scenic Canyon Regional Park covering 75 hectares on the eastern fringe of Kelowna contains portions of this landscape that has resulted from a surprising variety of earth processes (Figure 22).

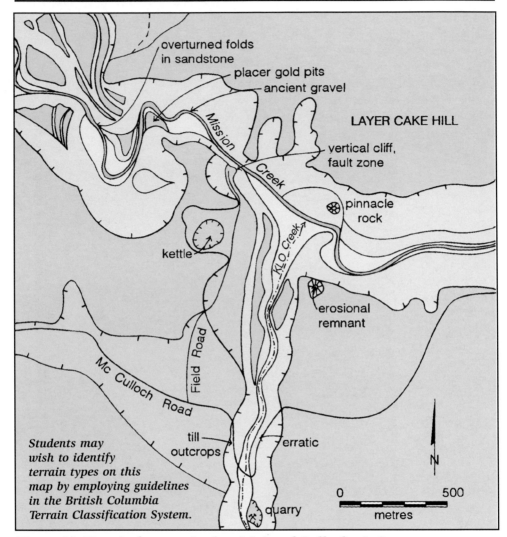

Figure 22: Terrain features in the vicinity of Gallagher's Canyon.

Layer Cake Hill

One of the most striking geologic features in the park is the layering in Layer Cake Hill, an "andesitic" lava flow or flows dated at about fifty million years old (Eocene Epoch). At least thirty two "layers" are exposed in a precipitous rock wall over two hundred and ten metres high along the northern edge of Gallagher's Canyon. The cause of the layering remains a subject of heated debate amongst geologists (see Stop 1, the Hardrock Trail, Appendix B).

Plate 17: A westerly view of the curious layering of volcanic rocks making up Layer Cake Hill. A possible explanation for this is given in the field trip "Hardrock Trail" in Appendix B.

Folded Sandstone Strata

On the north and south sides of Mission Creek in the western part of Gallagher's Canyon are folded beds of siltstone, sandstone and conglomeratic sandstone belonging to the White Lake Formation of Eocene age (Plate 18, also Plate 3).

These contain abundant fossil plant remains. Locally the sandstone has been moulded into symmetrical hoodoo-like sculptures, and caverns have been scooped out of the sandstone by stream erosion. Some caverns eroded into altered volcanics on the south side of the creek were used by the early Chinese gold miners as large ovens; the rocks at creek level still show the black sooty path of the smoke from these ovens.

Plate 18: Folded and overturned sandstone of the White Lake Formation in Gallagher's Canyon provides insight into the mountain building forces that once affected the Kelowna area.

Fault Zone

Plate 19: A view of a very steep gorge at Gallagher's Canyon taken from the base of Pinnacle Rock. The steep dark cliff is the same as that shown from stream level in Plate 2 and is composed of altered volcanics in a major fault zone.

Mission Creek at one point flows along an easterly trending fault or rupture zone in the bedrock that separates fifty million year old rocks on the north side of the creek from metamorphic rocks that are probably two billion years old on the south. This fault apparently offsets the Okanagan Lake fault (see Chapter Four).

Glacial Deposits and Ancient Gravels

At the Canyon exit the creek has also eroded through eighty metres of glacial material revealing ancient river gravels deposited on bedrock during preglacial time or during an interglacial period (Plate 20).

Plate 20: Rusty gravel outcrops at the exit of Gallagher's Canyon. It may be the only outcrop of the Rutland aquifer in the area, and the source of most of the gold in the creek flats below.

This ancient river valley represents an entirely different drainage pattern compared to the present, and may be the only outcrop of the locally important Rutland aquifer (see Chapter Twelve). Also, the gravels may be the main source of placer gold found in Mission Creek because gold was never found in economic quantities upstream from the canyon. Gold can still be panned in the creek gravel and in bedrock fractures downstream from this ancient river bed.

Thick sequences of glacial deposits are well exposed in other spots in the Canyon and reveal details of repeated glacial advance and retreat over the last 50,000 years or so. Terraces adjacent to the stream (Plate 19) represent former levels of deposition along the edges of glacial lakes some 10,000 years ago. Since that time Mission Creek has rapidly carved a deep canyon through the soft glacial sediments.

Pinnacle Rock

Pinnacle Rock, a curious spire-like landform near the base of Layer Cake Hill (front cover) is composed of the same layered volcanic rock as the Hill itself.

Although Pinnacle Rock may be an erosional remnant its formation is open to question. Aerial photos show that locally there are gaping vertical fractures in the hill. It is therefore possible that Pinnacle Rock slipped off the side of the escarpment as a block glide feature during downcutting of the valley by Mission Creek. Alternatively, Pinnacle Rock may simply be an erosional remnant carved out by deglaciation meltwater plunging into Mission Creek from KLO Creek.

Till Outcrops; The Descent Into KLO Creek (10)

Just past Field Road, McCulloch Road plunges down into the KLO Creek Valley (Figure 23). On descent there are outcrops of massive gray glacial till in the road cut which are amongst the best in the area (see also Plate 14). These poorly sorted and unstratified sediments contrast sharply with most glacial deposits in the Kelowna area which tend to be water-lain silts or water-worked sands and gravels.

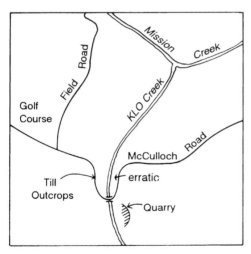

Figure 23. Location of Quarry, Till Outcrops and Erratic along McCulloch Road.

Quarry, Shuswap Rocks (11)

The oldest rocks in British Columbia are well exposed in a quarry at the bottom of KLO Creek valley. The distinctly banded rocks in the quarry walls are high grade metamorphic rocks (Monashee Group) of the Shuswap Terrane. Such banded rocks are known as gneisses (Plate 21).

Different coloured bands in the rock contain different minerals. Dark bands are enriched with a mineral known as hornblende, and lighter bands contain an abundance of feldspars such as microcline. Notice the stretched quartz veins in many samples on the quarry floor. Structures such as these indicate that the rocks have been subject to tremendous forces. The layering and segregation of these minerals were caused by extreme heat and pressure which completely changed the original rock type.

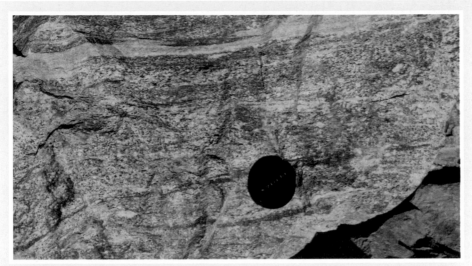

Plate 21: Gneiss belonging to the Shuswap Metamorphic Complex or Monashee Gneiss, the oldest rock in British Columbia. Also, see Stop 2 of the "Hardock Trail" field trip, Appendix B.

It is these features of the rock that indicate to geologists that the rock has been deeply buried. In fact, the current interpretation is that these rocks were originally granite and formed the edge of the early continental core of North America. Movement along the Okanagan Fault in Eocene time brought them to the surface. This rock is perhaps 2.0 billion years old, the oldest in British Columbia. The age is based on radiometric dating of similar rocks near Revelstoke (see also Stop 2, the Hardrock Trail, Appendix B).

Plate 22: Little White Mountain, the highest point in the Kelowna area, provides a backdrop for the Kettle Valley Railway that winds along the edge of the upland. Mine Hill is in the foreground, and the view is from the Scotty Creek area looking south-southeast.

Kettle Valley Railway (12)

Along with being a historical treasure-trove (see Sanford, 1978), an engineering feat of high rank, and providing breathtaking scenery, the abandoned Kettle Valley Railway between Myra Station and the Bellevue Trestle provides some spectacular geology as well. There are extensive outcrops of the Precambrian Monashee Gneiss (Shuswap rocks) and textbook-calibre outcrops of Miocene-Pliocene Chilcotin basalt unconformably overlying the gneiss and locally covering stream gravel. Locations of these features appear in Figure 19, and a photo of the landscape with Little White Mountain in the background is given in Plate 22.

History of the Kettle Valley Railway

A thin line through the forest far up on the hillside overlooking Kelowna is the only visible suggestion of the right-of-way of the Kettle Valley Railway. It was built by the Canadian Pacific Railway Company, and others, during the period 1901 to 1916. Construction was under the supervision of Andrew McCulloch (born in 1864), a remarkable Canadian engineer. The line operated from 1916 to 1962, hauling freight and resources between the Kootenays and the Pacific coast. It records a most intriguing and interesting saga of the development of British Columbia, a "magnificent irrationality" to quote Beth Hill, a local historian. Now abandoned, it is the focus of a strong and determined group of railway buffs, historians, hiking enthusiasts and others who are aiming to preserve its 500 kilometre corridor as a biking, skiing and hiking linear park.

The right-of-way of the Kettle Valley Railway, nearly 1,000 metres above Kelowna, can be accessed by taking the Myra Forest Access Road off McCulloch Road, or by following June Springs Road in East Kelowna. Between these two points the Kettle Valley Railway offers spectacular views of Kelowna and Okanagan Lake and impressive panoramas of deep canyons such as the two forks of KLO Creek, formerly known as Canyon Creek, and historically referred to as Myra Canyon. This section along the old grade contains sixteen high trestles that are engineering masterpieces, and two rock bound tunnels one of which is over 100 metres long. The largest trestle at Bellevue Creek is of steel construction 220 metres long and 55 metres high, but most are wooden. Walking or biking across these chasms can be an unnerving and chilling experience. Rock tunnels are somewhat hazardous. Rehabilitation of the trestles by community service groups and a great number of benefactors started in 1993. If one is cautious, this section of the KVR is perhaps one of the most enjoyable outings in the whole Okanagan Valley.

East Kelowna Fan (13)

The peaceful orchards, hobby ranches and equestrian centres of East Kelowna are situated on terrain similar in origin, though formed slightly earlier than the

Rutland Terraces. The first phase of meltwater coming out of Mission Creek valley, after diversion around Layer Cake Hill, formed a delta in East Kelowna (see cross-section, Figure 40, Chapter Thirteen). As glacial Lake Penticton drained and the once ice-laden land rose in response to unloading, Mission Creek dissected the delta. Eventually the creek established its present channel to the north leaving a series of near-dry valleys such as the "Gulley Road", marking the courses of these early stream channels in East Kelowna.

Beach Deposit, Crawford Estates (14)

Crawford Estates is situated on a high outwash gravel terrace marking the maximum height to which glacial Lake Penticton rose. The only well developed glacial Lake Penticton beach deposit in the Kelowna area occurs on the rim of this terrace. The deposit can be viewed to the west of Westridge Road (beachfront property) overlooking a large gravel pit which exposes the internal structure of the wave-built beach deposit (Plate 23). Part of this sand deposit was reworked into dunes by eolian(wind) activity. This is an important geologic landmark and could hold evidence of the first human activity in the Okanagan Valley (e.g. charcoal from camp fires or stone implements and tools may form middens buried beneath the sand). Unfortunately the locality is threatened by future development.

Other features in this area include Crawford Falls (30) and Bellevue Creek Canyon (29).

Plate 23: Looking like a desert, sand representing a beach at the highest level of glacial Lake Penticton parallels Westridge Road in Crawford Estates. Hayman Ridge and Okanagan Lake are in the background.

Oil Well Fiasco

In the early thirties the Okanagan Oil and Gas Company Limited announced plans to drill for oil at Kelowna. The promoters raised money from local businessmen to drill a series of wells just off Lakeshore Drive where it crosses Mission Creek. At least one hole was drilled through unconsolidated glacial sediments to a depth of nearly 1,000 metres, finally hitting a granitic type of rock (probably the Monashee Gneiss). Investors are still waiting for the oil to be turned on.

THE KELOWNA COURIER

AND OKANAGAN ORCHARDIST

Kelowna, British Columbia, Thursday, September 3rd, 1931

BORE OF OIL WELL BELOW SEA LEVEL

Indications Are Promising And Natural Gas Is Expected Within Next Eight Hundred Feet

Drilling was resumed at Kelowna Oil Well No. 1 on August 25th, the day after the casing was set, and a depth of 1,770 feet has now been attained. Sea level was passed at 1,737 feet. Mr. Julius Rickert, the geologist of the Okanagan Oil & Gas Co., Ltd., has waited patiently for sea level to be reached, and the formations encountered at that point verify his prediction and strengthen his opinion that natural gas will be encountered at about 2,500 feet or less.

There are considerable showings of gas, as well as oil seepage, and it is confidently expected that, on account of the greater depth, fewer troubles will be met in drilling, owing to lessening of possibilities of water and caving conditions, the rock formations now being more stratified.

The dogged perseverance shown by the founders of the enterprise in the face of many disheartening setbacks and delays is arousing keen interest and sympathy throughout the province and the Okanagan in general, as it is being recognized that genuine effort is being made to prove for once and for all the oil and gas possibilities of a formation which is not confined to the Kelowna district and therefore is of vast importance to the province in general. It is to be hoped that the sympathy will be translated into material terms of cash support, without which the undertaking cannot be carried to a conclusion. So far, the people of the Kelowna district and of other communities in the Okanagan have given a fair measure of assistance, but further funds will be required to make a thorough test, and any appeal made by the Company should meet with a liberal response.

Plate 24: A share certificate of the Kelowna Oil and Gas Co. Ltd., proving there were many optimists in Kelowna. A news article dated Thursday, September 3rd, 1931, from The Kelowna Daily Courier and Okanagan Orhardist" is also reproduced here, along with a photo of the "Kelowna Oil Well". These items were supplied through the courtesy of the Kelowna Museum.

Lambly Creek Basalt, Lakeview (15)

For about two kilometres south of the floating bridge, on the west side of Okanagan Lake, are lava flows belonging to the 762,000 year old Lambly Creek valley basalt (Plates 6 and 7). At least three separate flows outcrop in the steep escarpment paralleling the lake. Locally the basalt contains white calcareous fragments, apparently representing soft sediment picked up by the lava as it flowed. The sediment could hold valuable information on Okanagan climate at the time of basalt extrusion.

Kalamoir Regional Park (16)

The narrow road down to Kalamoir Regional Park, accessed from Collens Hill Road, affords close up views of dacite, a kind of volcanic rock that also makes up much of Mt. Boucherie. At this location the dacite forms contorted columns similar to those commonly observed in basaltic lava flows. Outcrops of conglomerate near the bottom of the road are representative of the White Lake Formation.

Mount Boucherie Columns (17)

Mount Boucherie is likely part of a former lava dome that dominated the landscape 50 million years ago. It has been carved and moulded by repeated glacial advances but remains a prominent geologic landmark in the Kelowna area. High on its eastern flank the mountain is seen to be made up of folded volcanic flows composed of dacite. The rocks also display columnar structure. The forest below the mountain is littered with large columnar blocks of dacite, resembling scattered ruins of an ancient temple and a forgotten civilization (see Plate 37, Appendix A).

Sandstone Cavities (18)

A spectacular cliff of White Lake Formation conglomerate occurs at the junction of Boucherie Road and Old Boucherie Road (Plate 25). Some parts of the 20 metre high cliff have been preferentially eroded producing numerous cavities. Fresh rocks at the base of the cliff show that the differential weathering is the result of oval areas in the conglomerate, known as concretions, being cemented together with the mineral calcite. Quartz cement holds the remainder of the rock together. Over the centuries mildly acidic rain water running over the outcrop has dissolved away the calcite allowing the contained boulders and pebbles to fall out of the cliff (see also Stop 5, the Hardrock Trail, Appendix B).

Plate 25: Conglomerate of the White Lake Formation is exposed in a scenic outcrop at the junction of Boucherie Road and old Boucherie Road in the Lakeview area.

McDougall Creek Fan (18)

McDougall Creek alluvial fan dominates two kilometres of the west shoreline of Okanagan Lake below Mount Boucherie (Figures 13 and 19). The fan was deposited perhaps six or seven thousand years ago in response to extensive erosion in the McDougall Creek watershed. This potentially powerful stream has in the past moved large boulders and formed hazardous "debris flows" that today would cause extensive damage. There remains some potential for flooding during extreme climatic events.

Varved Clay, Boucherie and Gellatly Roads (19)

The deep roadcuts along Boucherie Road and on Gellatly Road between the lake and Highway 97 at Westbank allow more views of varved clay formed in glacial Lake Penticton. This terrace correlates with that in Kelowna.

Glen Canyon Regional Park, Powers Creek, Glenrosa Area (20)

Although it is a steep trail, the climb down into Glen Canyon Regional Park is rewarding (Figure 24). Glacial outwash escaping down Powers Creek valley eroded a steep walled 100 metre canyon through massive conglomeratic beds of the White Lake Formation (Plate 5). Locally, thin coal beds can be seen in these ancient deltaic-like deposits along the canyon walls. Since deposition the rock layers have been tilted by tectonic forces and thus are no longer horizontal.

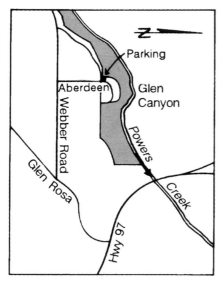

Figure 24

Coal Beds, White Lake Formation (21).

Coal outcrops as thin beds in the White Lake Formation across from Gorman Bros. Lumber Ltd. lumber mill. (See Stop 4, Hardrock Trail field trip, Appendix B).

Kelowna Bog (22)

The Kelowna bog is located just south of the airport, and is the subject of a special section in this book (see Chapter Six, Figure 16).

Plate 26: Long linear ridges of moraine form distinctive features of the Okanagan Valley near Sunset Ranch golf course (foreground). These are called lateral moraines.

Other Glacial Features

Lateral Moraine (23) and Drumlins

Linear ridges of moraine are easily visible along Okanagan Valley east of the airport in the vicinity of the Sunset Ranch golf course (Plate 26). These features formed at the edge of the Fraser Glacier as it stagnated along the valley and are called lateral moraines. Many are over one kilometre in length and are locally cut by dry valleys in places representing former meltwater channels.

Plate 27: Hard gneissic bedrock of Okanagan Mountain Park displays streamlined glacially abraded landforms and well formed drumlins in this eastward view from Hardy Creek.

Drumlins, carved at the base of a glacier, are common in the bedrock of Okanagan Mountain Park. Deeply scoured bedrock and drumlin forms can be seen looking across the lake from Highway 97 between Peachland and Summerland (Plate 27).

Black Knight Mountain (24)

Black Knight Mountain is a giant roche moutonnée, carved and plucked at the base of a southeastward moving glacier. The mountain is made of volcanic rock related to the same volcano that forms Layer Cake Hill. It is one of the most prominent landforms in the valley (Plate 28).

Plate 28: Black Knight Mountain has been molded by an overiding glacier into a giant roche moutonnée. This view shows the western side of this local landmark.

Eskers and Kames (25)

An intricate group of ice-contact landforms known as eskers and kames occur in the Black Mountain area south of Highway 33, in the vicinity of the rodeo grounds. Some of these deposits are presently being mined for gravel; this complex of unique landforms appears threatened by future development.

Other features of geologic interest not all described here include numbers 26 to 35 shown in Figure 19. Readers are invited to explore these and do their own geologic interpretation based on the information in this book. The authors would appreciate being informed of any other feature of geologic interest for future editions or to facilitate public awareness.

CHAPTER 9

GEOLOGIC HAZARDS IN THE OKANAGAN VALLEY

Geologic hazards are natural processes that can be damaging to private property, structures and/or human life. Five major types include landslides, sinkholes, floods, earthquakes and volcanic eruptions.

Landslides

Landslides are facts of life in British Columbia, and the Okanagan is no exception. Landslide is a general term used to describe the down-slope movement of soil, rock and organic materials, wet or dry, and the landform that results. There are various types of landslides; main types are shown in Figure 25.

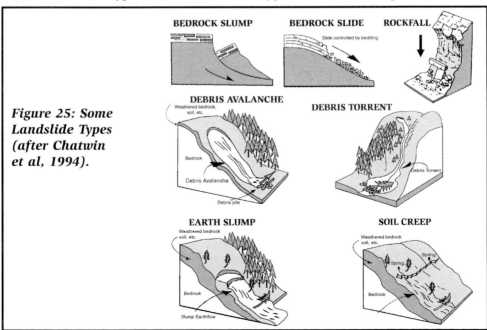

Figure 25: Some Landslide Types (after Chatwin et al, 1994).

Causes of Landslides

Landslides are often caused by more than one factor. Undercutting of a slope by a river is the most common. This was the main cause of a spectacular rotational slump which occurred in October 1984 on Mission Creek nine kilometres east of Kelowna along Highway 33 (Plate 29).

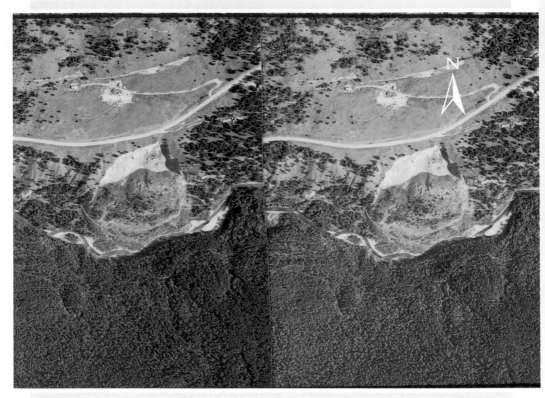

Plate 29: This is a stereo-pair of the Mission Creek rotational slump nine kilometres east of Kelowna and just south of Highway 33. A stereoscope is required to see the terrain in 3-dimensions. (Air photos 30BCC 92092 – 3 & 4 reprinted courtesy of Province of British Columbia, Surveys and Resource Mapping Branch.)

Approximately 500 metres of the north bank of the creek valley failed and completely blocked Mission Creek. The thunder clap sound produced during failure was heard as far away as Orchard Park shopping mall 10 kilometres to the west (Don Dobson, personal communication). This landslide involved over ten million tonnes of material and nearly destroyed a portion of Highway 33. It is an important geologic landmark and a vivid reminder of the hazard that exists on some Okanagan slopes.

Another cause of landslides is the addition of water either from prolonged rainfall, melting snow, or groundwater seepage. Water pressure builds up in sediment pores causing a loss of strength and, ultimately, failure. Terrain underlain by silt and clay of glacial Lake Penticton is particularly sensitive to pore pressure build-up along slopes. Many slopes in the Kelowna area, such as near the base of Knox Mountain, along the Rutland Terrace and along Swamp Road are character-ized by earth flows and slumps. For example slumping occurred on a terrace at the northern end of Gordon Drive on August 21, 1993 (Mountain Avenue slide). Three houses were damaged when water-saturated silt and clay extruded at the base of a terrace slope; backyards of two houses dropped six to twelve metres as a result (Plate 30).

Plate 30: This person's backyard and patio on Mountain Avenue at the end of Gordon Drive in Kelowna took a "down elevator" the night of August 21, 1993. No one was injured.

Landslides have been caused by the unintentional or accidental release of excess irrigation water on orchards above steep slopes. This was the apparent cause of a slide on Lakeshore Drive at Summerland during 1992 and in another location here in 1970 which destroyed three homes and killed one person (Evans, 1982). Over a dozen large slides have occurred along Okanagan Lake since 1930 and some along Osoyoos and Skaha Lakes. Large silt slumps still occur unpre-dictably along Highway 97 especially between Summerland and Penticton.

Earthquakes are the most widely known cause of landslides. Examples can be cited for many parts of the world. Although Kelowna has a low earthquake risk, whenever a slide occurs investigators always check to see if it may coincide with the time of a recorded earthquake.

Clearcut logging and forest access roads contribute to the probability of land-slide activity in some localities, although forest companies are working hard to reduce this hazard. In upland clearcut areas more rainfall seeps into the ground which in turn may increase pore pressure on adjacent slopes as water tries to escape. These conditions may persist until the clearcut has hydrologically regener-ated. Surface water runoff also increases in clearcut areas potentially raising the extent of erosion, undercutting of banks, and the probability of debris transport during rain storms, especially if access roads are not carefully constructed, main-tained or deactivated.

THE ROLE OF GROUNDWATER

The influence of groundwater on slope stability is not commonly appreciated by the general public. The addition of water to slope-forming materials has two major consequences. First, the soil becomes more buoy-ant; this reduces the strength of the soil. Second, depending on the pres-sure imposed by the groundwater build-up in combination with the type of soil on the slope and the actual slope angle, buoyant forces and pore pres-sure may combine to overwhelm the natural resistance of the soil to gravity and a failure occurs. In some cases the failure takes the form of an explo-sion, like the popping of a champagne cork. Even if the pop-out on a slope is small, the resulting small debris flow can trigger a much larger failure downslope, or it may "snowball" into a larger one. The former happened in the Belgo Creek debris avalanche in the Joe Rich District slide in June of 1990. Runoff from a poorly maintained forest access road drained into a sensitive part of a slope that was naturally somewhat unstable.

The Anatomy of a Debris Avalanche

The Belgo Creek debris avalanche thirty kilometres east of Kelowna occurred on June 12, 1990, in a poorly to moderately drained till mantled depressional swale on the western slope of Belgo Creek valley. The landslide resulted in a water-charged debris avalanche over 1.5 kilometres long. Seventeen terrain units defining the slide have been recognized (Ministry of Forests, 1990, and Cass *et al*, 1992). Five debris torrents also occurred in the general area (Figure 26).

The main avalanche developed from three small related debris flows on a steep water saturated slope. These minor events and accompanying tree falls in turn triggered the main flow, the head scarp of which had received an unusual amount of runoff due to disrupted drainage on a forestry access road.

A forty-two day period preceding the mass movement events was the wettest on record. An intense storm within 24 hours of the slide combined with snow melt is believed to have created saturated conditions in the surficial materials and high pore pressure in both the surficial material and underlying fractured bedrock. This caused an explosive outburst of surficial materials and loose

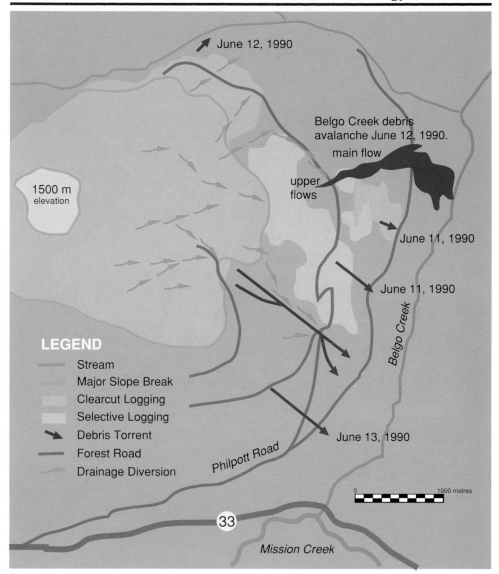

June 12, 1990

Belgo Creek debris
avalanche June 12, 1990.

main flow

upper
flows

1500 m
elevation

June 11, 1990

June 11, 1990

Belgo Creek

LEGEND
— Stream
— Major Slope Break
■ Clearcut Logging
■ Selective Logging
➤ Debris Torrent
— Forest Road
➤ Drainage Diversion

Philpott Road

June 13, 1990

0   1000 metres

33

Mission Creek

*Figure 26: Map of the Belgo Creek Debris Failure Area, Philpott Road,
Joe Rich District.*

bedrock where slopes are in the order of 65-75% (30 to 40 degrees) and springs
emanated from the bedrock. Spray from the top flow scar which is only 1.5
metres in diameter, splattered nearby trees three metres up their trunks.

Velocity of the main slide has been estimated at 10 metres per second and
involved 23,000 cubic metres of soil, forest debris and a large quantity of water
(Cass *et al*, 1992). A house was demolished and three people lost their lives.

Plate 31: Part of the debris at the base of the Belgo Creek debris avalanche is shown here. The debris pile here includes a demolished house in which three people lost their lives.

Brenda Pit Slide

A spectacular rock avalanche on the west wall in the Brenda Mines pit occurred April 9, 1990, and ended production. The failure was expected and had

Plate 32: A rockslide on the west wall of the pit at Brenda Mines Ltd., shown here, terminated production in 1990. Photo courtesy of Brenda Mines Ltd.

been closely monitored for months. Approximately eight million tonnes of rock filled the bottom of the pit to a depth of over 30 metres. Cause of the slide was structural failure and high groundwater pressure on the 300 metre high wall with an average slope of about 80% (40 degrees). The slide caused a small earthquake, recorded at the Pacific Geoscience Center in Sydney, BC.

Landslide Risk

The public is generally unaware of landslide risk areas which is unfortunate. Statistically, large and infrequent landslides contribute less to personal and property damage than smaller more frequent landslides in populated regions. Increased public awareness and more frequent consultation with qualified geotechnical personnel prior to development could limit activities that result in the undercutting of slopes, eliminate the placement of fill on steep slopes, emphasize the necessity of proper drainage, and prevent building construction near unstable slope crests.

Stage One

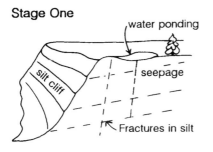

Stage Two

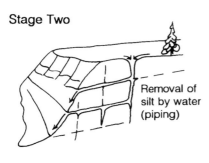

Stage Three

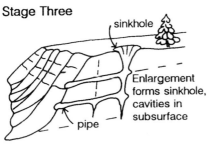

Sinkholes

Sinkholes in the Okanagan result from a process known as piping. Piping occurs when water seeping along vertical and/or horizontal fractures in silt interacts with the tiny sediment particles causing a collapse of the structure holding the silt particles together. The silt particles become mobilized by water along a thin tubular pipe where the fracture originally occurred. With time the pipe enlarges, caving occurs and the ground collapses due to the extrusion of silt along the pipe. Sinkholes are common in the bluffs of glacial Lake Penticton sediments due to their unconsolidated silty composition (Figure 27). They are especially well developed in the Sage Mesa area near Penticton.

Sinkhole formation destroys foundation conditions. Any ground depression underlain by Lake Penticton strata should be thoroughly analyzed before

Figure 27: Sketches showing stages in the formation of sinkholes by piping in silts of glaciolacustrine sediment.

construction. Filling sinkholes is not a long term remedy. The hazard can be considerably increased by uncontrolled irrigation or even backyard watering.

Floods

Flooding of property in Kelowna, although commonly attributed to "too much rain" often has more complicated origins of both human and natural contrivance. Much of the city is built on a flat delta that emerged above lake level over the last part of the Holocene. In many places the water table is less than a metre below the surface and can be higher when runoff into Okanagan Lake exceeds the controlled outlet capacity at Penticton and Okanagan Falls causing the lake and water table levels to rise. In addition the Kelowna flatland is a huge groundwater discharge zone, receiving water that infiltrates from the surrounding highland. During rain storms water level is easily affected first by runoff and then by a rise in the groundwater table. This results in flooding of septic tile fields, basements, and in extreme cases, overtopping of stream channels.

Mission Creek supplies one third of the annual runoff to Okanagan Lake and has a notorious past history for flooding. The stream has now been so channelized across the flats to prevent water from breaching the banks, that even the Kokanee may be finding the creek somewhat unrecognizable. Urbanization masks the natural sinuous channels the stream used to follow less than two hundred years ago and to which it would return to without human intervention. Several reservoirs have been constructed in the watershed (see Chapter Twelve) and help control runoff. Thus the flooding threat is presently diminished but Mission Creek may strike again.

Plate 33: Mission Creek on a summer day is a placid pleasant stream. However, it drains one of the largest watersheds in the Okanagan Valley and supplies one third of the annual runoff to Okanagan Lake. Its potential for flooding should not be underestimated.

Like Mission Creek all streams entering the valley have alluvial fans or deltas associated with them (e.g. Fintry Creek, McDougall Creek, Trepanier Creek, Scotty Creek, etc.). These areas may be at risk from flooding particularly during a climatic extreme event, and unfortunately tend to be urbanization sites. The July 1993 flash flood on Scotty Creek damaged residences and the Sunset Ranch golf course illustrating one type of hazard. This flood was caused by failure of an abandoned beaver dam high up in the watershed!

The public can hardly be aware of all potential flooding hazards. However, watershed users have a responsibility to know of watershed sensitivities, to monitor activities and carefully plan upstream terrain development. It is important to ensure minimal risks to downstream facilities and people, and strive to maintain water quality.

Inadequately designed or maintained storm drainage systems can also cause "unexpected" floods. Urbanization creates impermeable surfaces such as paved streets that, during storms, increase the availability and speed of runoff water and locally elevates soil infiltration. Hazards develop due mainly to enhanced surface erosion. Ponding and infiltration leads to increased subsurface pore pressure and landslides. In addition, runoff from urbanized areas carries far more pollutants to lakes and streams than water handled by sewage treatment plants. Preservation of our surface water and groundwater quality requires new ways of dealing with storm water drainage, and a policy for retention basins in new subdivisions is now being enforced.

Earthquakes

Earthquakes are a potential hazard in British Columbia. They are caused when stresses build up in the earth much like what happens when an elastic band is stretched. Eventually the earth's crust suddenly ruptures forming a fault, or break in the crust, and instantaneously releasing the stored energy. The energy travels through the earth as waves similar to the waves produced by a pebble dropped into water. These waves are powerful and may cause widespread destruction.

Plate tectonics helps us understand why these stresses build up in the earth's crust and why British Columbia is at risk. Figure 6 shows the principal tectonic "plates" on the Pacific coast. The plates are colliding, sliding past or moving away from one another and it is near these plate boundaries where most earthquakes originate. Plate movement is very slow, typically only a few millimetres to centimetres a year but over time energy can accumulate, and its sudden release may cause a mighty earthquake.

Kelowna Earthquake Risk

Scientists believe that coastal British Columbia may be overdue for a major earthquake. Much of the earthquake hazard for the Okanagan comes from the potential in the Lower Mainland or coastal zone (Ernie Naesgaard, personal communication). The distribution and intensity of earthquakes in the Okanagan shown in Figure 28 illustrate that the hazard potential for the Okanagan is much less than for the Lower Mainland. This reflects our distance from the plate boundaries in the offshore (Figure 6). For example a 1946 earthquake on Vancouver Island registered 7.3 on the Richter Scale. It produced a high level of shaking capable of moderate building damage and set off landslides for 200 kilometres

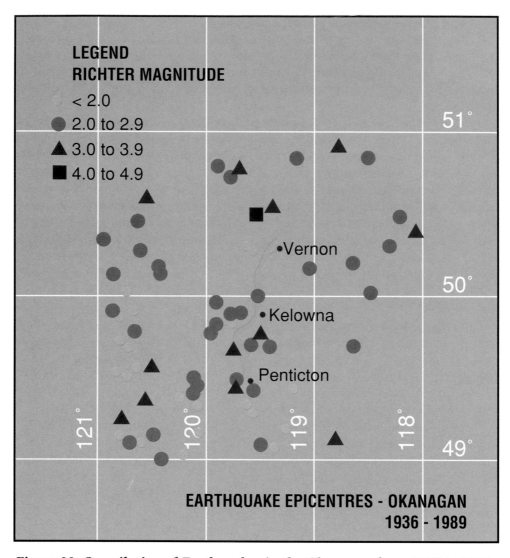

Figure 28: Compilation of Earthquakes in the Okanagan from 1936 to 1989. The largest was northwest of Vernon in 1936 at 4.5 Richter (Data courtesy of Pacific Geoscience Center, Sidney, British Columbia). The Richter scale is gradually being phased out of use and replaced with a new scale based on magnitude ("M" scale) of energy released. The two scales are very similar for quakes less than 7.0.

around its origin (epicenter) near Courtenay. Kelowna, 400 kilometres away, may have experienced a very low level of shaking during this event.

The potential for a major earthquake originating in the Okanagan appears very low. However, no specific work has been done but numerous scientists have examined sediment of Holocene age (the last 10,000 years) in exposures throughout the Okanagan Valley, and there is no report that these sediments have been offset by movement along a fault. Earthquake activity in historical times in the Okanagan has been restricted to minor shaking with earthquake magnitudes in the range of 2.0 to 4.5 Richter, as shown in Figure 28. Nevertheless it is sobering to realize that the Okanagan fault zone with numerous related faults is a major zone of weakness in the Earth's crust, and runs directly beneath Kelowna.

Although some very loose sediments in the Kelowna area could liquefy even during very small disturbances, such as the placement of berms on certain spots in Okanagan Lake, it would take an earthquake with a magnitude of 7.5 Richter at Vancouver to cause potential liquefaction of most liquefaction-prone sediments at Kelowna. The estimated frequency of such an event affecting Kelowna may be once every ten thousand years on the basis of existing geologic evidence. This is important because Kelowna cannot afford to have any shaking going on. Shaking causes water saturated silts and fine sands to liquefy, and Kelowna largely sits on these sediment types. The potential for liquefaction is one reason why engineers did not build a suspension bridge across Lake Okanagan; a floating bridge was constructed instead at a much lower cost.

The probability may be very low but the potential ramifications of high level shaking are daunting. Depending on site conditions, buildings on the flats of Kelowna could be damaged or destroyed, houses would settle or sink, landslides could be triggered. A large earthquake centred in the Okanagan Valley could generate giant destructive waves in Okanagan Lake causing havoc and probably loss of life along its heavily populated shore. Fortunately, the possibility of this appears extremely low.

Earthquake Prediction

Earthquake prevention is presently impossible as is accurate prediction. However, the destructive consequences can be reduced by proper planning, appropriate building site selection, structural design through geologic and geotechnical studies, an informed public, and a prepared emergency response team.

Volcanic Eruptions

Major periods of volcanic eruption that affected Kelowna in the geologic past were described in earlier portions of the book. Although there are three different active volcanic belts within British Columbia that produced over 100 eruptions during the Quaternary Period, the Okanagan area has been largely, though not entirely, inactive and minimally affected.

Volcanic Ash Falls at Kelowna Since the Ice Age

Local surficial sediment deposits formed over the last 10,000 years contain at least four layers of volcanic ash. The oldest is the Mazama Ash derived from an explosion that formed Crater Lake in Oregon 6,600 years ago (Plate 34).

Plate 34: A small landslide has exposed a 2 to 3 centimetre layer of volcanic ash (white band) in this photo of a cutbank along Mission Creek near Philpott Road east of Kelowna. This is likely Mazama Ash, dated at 6,600 years before the present.

Just south of the Kelowna airport the Mazama Ash is over one metre thick where it accumulated in a depression {(22) in Figure 19, see also Figure 16}. Imagine the environmental impact of even a fraction of that ash fall would have on Kelowna today, and this from a source 700 kilometres away! Ash falls originated from Mt. St. Helens (Washington) 3,400 years ago, Mt. Meager (Bridge River, BC) 2,400 years ago, and again from Mt. St. Helens 508 years ago. The wind during the 1980 eruption of Mt. St. Helens was to the east and did not deposit ash in Kelowna. However, from recent studies it is apparent that, depending on wind direction, the probability of an ash fall at Kelowna from an explosive eruption of one or more of the numerous Cascade volcanoes is quite high for any year.

Lambly Creek Valley Lava Flows

The most recent volcanic eruption of a non-explosive nature in the Kelowna area was 760,000 years ago. It originated near Lambly Lake, at the headwaters of Bear Creek on the west side of Lake Okanagan. Several rivers of basaltic lava flowed down Bear Creek, turned south (possibly diverted by a valley glacier) and continued to Lakeview Heights (Figure 5, Plates 6 and 7). The Lambly Creek valley lava flow has been largely eroded by streams and glacial activity but remnants form the cliffs just south of the floating bridge. The vent for the flow has never been found. Chemical similarities between this lava flow and the Chilcotin Plateau lavas suggest that this infrequent and sporadic igneous activity which started 25 million years ago may still be possible today. There is little need to worry however, volcanism only occurs about once every million years, and the last explosive eruption at Kelowna was in the order of 50 million years ago.

Hot Spots in the Okanagan

Brief mention here of geothermal heat resources in the Okanagan serves to emphasize that the ancient volcanic centres have not entirely cooled (Figure 29). The Okanagan Valley from Winfield south is believed to have high potential as a geothermal heat source that could be used to heat buildings or generate electricity. Geothermal gradients beneath known volcanic piles range from 50° to 70° Celsius per kilometre of depth (Fairbank and Faulkner, 1992). In other words, a hole 2,000 metres deep could tap water with a temperature of 140° Celsius in some locations. However, recent testing west of Summerland and drilling at the base of Layer Cake Hill in Gallagher's Canyon have as yet not identified an economic energy source. Perhaps higher petroleum prices and hydro-electric costs will be required before the local geothermal heat potential is realized.

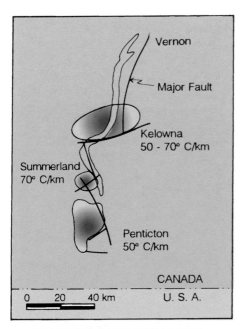

Figure 29: Geothermal heat is being generated at certain places in the Okanagan Valley as shown by temperature gradients given in this map (modified after Fairbank and Faulkner, 1992).

HOT SPOTS IN THE OKANAGAN

Kelowna Warm-Springs

by John D. Greenough

Few people know about them, but there are warm-springs up the KLO Creek valley ((31) in Figure 19). They are most accessible by driving up June Springs Road to the 1 km sign on the Forestry Service Road and then hiking northeast for about one hour along an old logging road and hiking trail.

Water from the springs crosses the hiking trail in a small ravine, and is easily identified by its bright orange color. The color results from exuberant algal growth and the precipitation of iron-bearing minerals. These features plus water temperatures of about 20 to 25 degrees Celsius discourage bathing. However, these temperatures probably reflect mixing of hot-spring water with colder surface and cool-spring waters. Temperatures as high as 29 degrees Celsius occur around seeps a few hundred metres up the ravine.

Perhaps the most fascinating geological aspect of the springs is the extensive tufa deposits that form a series of terraces with 10 metre-high benches at irregular intervals along the ravine. These deposits attest to the presence of prolonged hydrothermal (hot water) activity that could be thousands of years old and that may have been more productive in past times.

At present we can only speculate about the origin of the warm water. Possibly the ravine demarcates a fault in the ancient gneisses that outcrop along the walls of the gorge. Water originating deep in the earth could follow the fault to the surface. Possible heat sources include the earth's interior (temperature rises with depth in the earth) or a magma chamber. The spring does occur within the Kelowna hot spot as shown in Figure 29. Another hypothesis is that the water is flowing from gravel deposits underlying plateau basalts that are one to three million years old. These basalts outcrop along the Kettle Valley Railway bed just above the ravine and rumour has it that drill holes through similar basalts in the area encountered warm water in underlying gravel deposits.

CHAPTER 10

GEOTECHNICAL CONDITIONS IN THE KELOWNA AREA

Norm Williams and Murray A. Roed

The term geotechnical refers to the study and prediction of how bedrock, surficial deposits, groundwater, surface water and topographic conditions relate to construction of buildings, roads and utilities. Even a casual glance at the surficial geology map of the Kelowna area (Figure 13) suggests that the range of deposits presents demanding challenges to any geotechnical consultant advising on the use of the land. Conditions vary considerably and are briefly summarized.

Deltaic and Alluvial Fans

Extending roughly from Orchard Park to the lakefront Kelowna is situated on a thick sequence of interbedded organic material, clay, silt, sand and gravel deposited by ancestor channels, ponds and fans of Mill (Kelowna) Creek and Mission Creek. These sediments are loosely consolidated and are usually saturated within a few metres of the surface. The finer grained soils are loose and compressible and even for small buildings require special consideration for settlement and earthquake behavior.

Glacial Lake Sediments

Silt and clay deposited in glacial Lake Penticton are widespread in the area. These deposits can be found in Glenmore Valley, at Okanagan University College, along the base of Knox Mountain, along Swamp Road and Hartman Road, and in places in East Kelowna and KLO Road as well as numerous locations on the west side of the lake. These soils are hard clayey type sediments with some swelling potential. That is, when wet they swell, and when dried they shrink. Numerous incidents of settlement, cracking of foundations and basement slab displacements can be traced to the behavior of these soils under differing conditions.

Generally, for single family dwellings, these clayey soils should be removed to a certain depth and replaced with compacted granular materials that have good drainage. In some cases an alternate design should be considered.

Glacial Moraine Deposits

Moraine deposits include till (Plate 14), a dense mixture of clay, silt, sand and boulders, deposited directly from melting glacier ice, and stratified sand and gravel deposited by glacial meltwater. These surficial soils are most common at elevations above 500 metres. Construction and foundation problems are few since they are usually well drained, have high strength and are not compressible under normal loads. However, where drainage is poor and where slopes are involved these soils can be hazardous (see Chapter Nine).

Bedrock

A great variety of bedrock types occur in the Kelowna area as shown in Figure 5. Generally, bedrock does not offer many geotechnical problems unless the rock is fractured or loose, or if it is subject to rockfall, or some other form of failure. In many rock localities the greatest impact is economic in that the rock may have to be blasted which increases the cost of construction and introduces a potential hazard if blasts are not properly controlled.

Geotechnical Implications of the Floating Bridge

Opening of the Okanagan Floating Bridge, the longest in the world, by Princess Margaret in 1958 ended a ferry service that dated to 1904. Over 30,000 people attended the opening which also marked the first live televised event of CHBC-TV. The bridge cost 7.5 million dollars to construct. Along with its social, economic and political ramifications, it is a major geotechnical and structural

Plate 35: One of the anchors originally used for the Kelowna floating bridge is displayed in Anchor Park at the corner of Pandosy and Harvey Avenue.

engineering achievement (Pegush, 1957). The bridge is over three kilometres long, including approaches. It has a 640 metre long floating section consisting of twelve reinforced concrete pontoons rigidly connected to form one continuous pontoon. The pontoons are held in place by cables anchored seven metres into lake bottom sediments. One of the original concrete anchors, weighing 64 tonnes, is displayed at the corner of Harvey Avenue and Pandosy Street in downtown Kelowna (Plate 35). In the eastern section of the bridge a 79 metre lift span accommodates the passage of large boats.

Why build a floating bridge? A suspension bridge was designed originally but the highly compressible(soft) surficial sediments in the lake bottom ruled it out because there was no suitable layer in which piling could be practically and economically installed. There would also be a danger of liquefaction (loss of strength due to shaking) in the event of an earthquake. These deltaic and lacustrine sediments include soft layers, and are completely saturated. These bottom materials could not support a rock causeway either, which was also a design option. Thus geological conditions and economics necessitated a floating bridge. Additional crossing capability is now required, and all of the options are being re-evaluated including an update on earthquake hazards.

The Grand Okanagan Lake Front Resort

Clay, silt and sand associated with deltaic and lacustrine sedimentation also underlie a twelve storey hotel at the Grand Okanagan Lake Front Resort in downtown Kelowna (Figure 30).

Elaborate remedial measures were necessary to prepare this site for construction (Howie et al, 1994). Soils to depths of 55 metres were investigated by drilling and engineering tests. They were found to be compressible at depth, and an upper sand layer containing high silt content had potential for liquefaction.

The entire site was loaded with a ten metre high pile of soil to squeeze out water and force settlement of soft layers in the subsurface (Figure 30). This load was maintained for about one year in 1991 and served to consolidate the deep soils to an acceptable engineering standard. Vibro-compaction was then used to densify the upper sands at the site. Finally a "raft" slab of concrete 1.2 metres thick was placed to form the foundation of the structure and further limit long-term settlement of the subsoil. A six metre wide strip along the lakeshore was also densified to arrest potential lakeshore instability.

Geotechnical design for this development has resulted in settlement below predictions. It has prepared the soil to withstand the risk of an estimated 1 in 475 year shaking event due to an earthquake, and allowed the possibility of further development.

Historically the site of the Grand development first served as a ferry landing. Between 1900 and 1930 part of the site was used for waste disposal from a sawmill. Since then the shoreline has been continuously pushed into the lake by random filling and finally by a dyke built in 1986 and subsequently infilled.

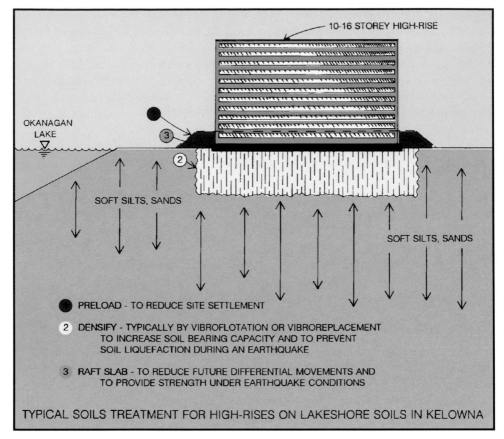

Figure 30: This sketch shows the various stages of site preparation for construction of the Grand Okanagan Hotel beside the lake in downtown Kelowna.

Okanagan University College

During excavation for foundations at the new Okanagan University College, across from the airport, clay subject to high swelling was encountered (Figure 31).

Final design was based on removal of over three metres of the clay and replacement with compacted sand and gravel. This acts as a thick "mat" foundation, and will insure that no settlement takes place even if there is minor swelling in the remaining clay soils at depth.

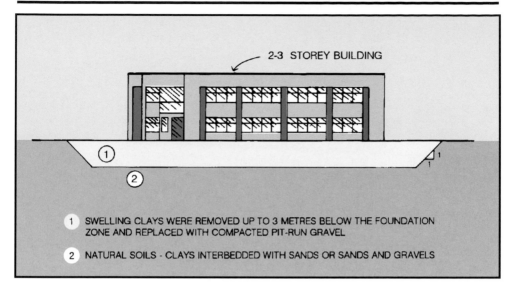

Figure 31: Foundation preparation for the north campus of the Okanagan University College is summarized in this sketch.

Other Conditions at Kelowna

The flat terrain of Kelowna is generally poorly drained. A high water table is characteristic and basement flooding is a common problem in many localities. Along Swamp Road and adjacent terrain, clayey soils have a high organic content which makes them subject to settlement and swelling. Consequently the road is warping, and some mass movement has also taken place. Construction of a stable road base in organic soils may require excavation and replacement with granular material or placement of fill with adequate drainage. Either way costs escalate.

Unusual soils occur in places. Near the Bernard Avenue overpass by Dr. Knox Middle School a 60 centimetre thick layer of diatomaceous earth was encountered in flood plain sediments. This probably represents deposition in an old pond related to a meander of one of the streams that used to cross the area.

CHAPTER 11

MINERAL RESOURCES

Mineral resources have played an important role in Kelowna's history. Just two years after Father Pandosy established his agricultural based Okanagan Mission in 1859, gold was discovered in Mission Creek, fueling early settlement in the valley. A silver mine at Beaverdell helped bring the Kettle Valley Railway into the area in the early 1900's and development of a molybdenum-copper deposit by Brenda Mines Ltd. poured millions of dollars into the local economy during the 1970's and 80's. A uranium deposit discovered at Lassie Lake south of Big White Mountain in 1977 did not bring more wealth into the local economy. However, it precipitated a moratorium on uranium mining and exploration in British Columbia which reflects the environmentally conscious attitudes of area residents a decade and a half ago. These four ore deposits represent the most important non-renewable mineral resource discoveries affecting Kelowna, apart from important sand and gravel aggregate resources. The geologic formation of these mineral resources, discovery and development are explored below.

Gold Mining, Gallagher's Canyon

When Father Pandosy founded the Okanagan Mission in 1859 on the floodplain of Mission Creek, the settlement was primarily an agricultural production centre, independent of fur trading or gold mining which were the historic economic targets of early explorers. Gold was first discovered in the Okanagan as early as 1833 by David Douglas, a botanist, who apparently panned some gold on a shore of Lake Okanagan according to historian Primrose Upton. Gold in Mission Creek valley at what is now known as Scenic Canyon Regional Park was discovered by one of Father Pandosy's original guides, William Peon (also spelled Pion), in 1861, the same year that the rich deposits at Williams Creek and Lightning Creek in the Cariboo were discovered, and long before the Klondike gold rush of the 1890's.

Placer mining continued at Mission Creek until about 1900 but work was sporadic and probably few made more than wages. Chinese miners also worked the stream valley for a period of time and left visible evidence of their activity. They always piled the rocks from their diggings in neat fence-like structures.

Dr. George M. Dawson, one of the most prominent scientists of the Geological Survey of Canada, and a pioneer in the annals of Canadian geology, visited the mine workings on Mission Creek in 1877. He reported only a few men still employed. Early miners apparently recovered two to three ounces of gold per day from the stream bed, and the gold was quite coarse.

Ed Aldredge, a Penticton historian, places the discovery of gold on Mission Creek as early as 1853 or even before. He also mentions that the late Alan Richardson of Penticton had a claim on Mission Creek, somewhere, as recently as the late 1970's.

Dan Gallagher was probably the most persistent miner. According to historians Lundy and Zoellner (1990), he pre-empted land in the canyon in 1898 and worked a claim up to the 1930's. He lived there as a recluse in a cabin, was in popular demand as a fiddler, and is rumored to have been a cattle rustler on occasion. His cabin burned, and its location is not known. Today the locality is known as Gallagher's Canyon which apparently includes the total length of rugged bedrock landscapes along Mission Creek.

THE BRENDA MINE

by Peter Peto and John Greenough

The Brenda Mine, about 60 kilometres southwest of Kelowna (Figure 32), has an interesting exploration and development history that underscores the perseverance and ingenuity of the Canadian mining industry. In the 1930's the Sandberg family of Kelowna discovered copper and molybdenum mineralization where the Brenda open-pit exists today. Bob Bechtel of Penticton re-discovered and staked the long-abandoned Sandberg workings in 1954, and optioned the property to Noranda following discussions with Bern Brynelson. Drilling in 1956 indicated an average ore grade of 0.21% copper and 0.03% molybdenum. These results enticed Kennecott Copper to join Noranda and carry out a systematic surface exploration program in 1957. Discouraging results saw the property returned to Bechtel with sufficient assessment work done to keep it in good standing for 10 years.

By 1964 the development of large-tonnage open pit mining methods in other places and increasing demand for molybdenum from the steel industry prompted Bern Brynelson, Morris Menzies and Mervin Davis to form a publicly traded company (Brenda Mines Ltd.) on the Vancouver Stock Exchange to carry out further exploration. Brenda Mines Ltd. in partnership with Nippon Mining of Japan undertook a $3.5 million mining feasibility program in 1965. This involved col-

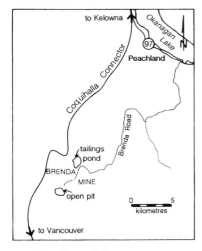

Figure 32: Location of the Brenda Mine.

lecting a 10,800 tonne bulk sample of the mineralized zone. The bulk sample was run through a 90 tonne per day mill to determine what percentage of the molybdenum and copper could be recovered from the ore.

Enthused by the results, Noranda bought a controlling interest in Brenda Mines Ltd. and financed construction of a $62.5 million mining operation in January of 1968. The ore body had proven reserves of 159.3 million tonnes grading 0.183% copper and 0.049% molybdenum making it the lowest grade Cu-Mo mine in the world! Thus, following 16 years of perseverance by Bechtel and as a result of the ingenuity of Noranda geologists and engineers, the Brenda ore body was mined profitably for the next 21 years.

Geology

The Brenda deposit occurs at the junction of two large igneous intrusions, the older is a diorite and the other a granodiorite (Soregaroli and Whitford, 1974). Both are part of a batholith that formed some 176 to 146 million years ago during the Jurassic Period (Figure 33). Similar rocks of this age are quite common in the Interior Mountain System Plateau (Peto, 1973). Molten rock forming the batholith intruded (was injected into) late Paleozoic to late Triassic (250 - 200 million years old) volcanic and sedimentary rocks. The intruded rocks have been "baked" or metamorphosed for a distance of 500 metres away from the granite contact. Detailed geologic mapping indicates that the Brenda ore deposit formed at the roof of the batholith near where it contacted older volcanic and sedimentary rocks (Rice, 1947). The ore body is cut by various other igneous rocks, many probably intruded during the Tertiary mountain building event. A period of prolonged uplift and erosion, including glaciation, following the Tertiary generated the deeply dissected valleys, gently rolling upland plateau and present-day bedrock outcrops pattern.

The ore body occupies an irregular area of 853 by 396 metres and extends downward more than 300 metres. The main ore minerals are sulphides; chalcopyrite (a copper, iron and sulphur mineral) and molybdenite (contains molybdenum and sulphur). These minerals, which represent less than 1% of the rock, are accompanied by variable amounts of pyrite (fool's gold), minor bornite (another copper mineral) and rarely sphalerite or galena (zinc and lead ore minerals respectively) together with the waste (gangue) minerals quartz, potassium feldspar, biotite, calcite and epidote.

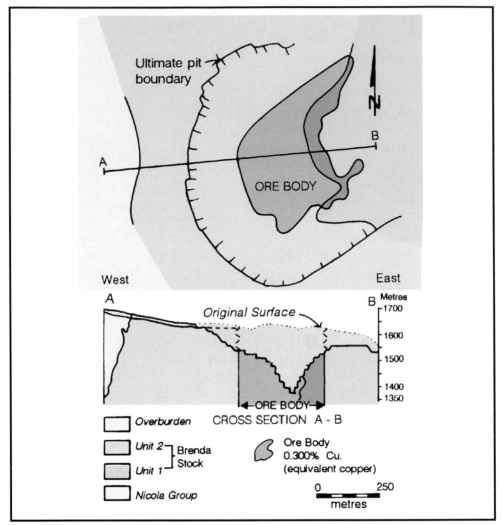

Figure 33: Geology of the Brenda Mine (after Soregaroli and Whitford, 1974).

The ore mineralization occurs in fracture-filling veins, typically 0.5 to 2.5 cm thick with the number and size of veins, and thus ore grade, increasing toward the centre of the deposit. At least five distinct stages of veining are recognized based on mineralogy of the veins.

Mineral Genesis

The Brenda deposit belongs to a class of ore deposits known as Copper-Molybdenum porphyries. These deposits form when a continent collides with ocean crust resulting in the ocean floor being shoved beneath the continent. This plate tectonic process is called subduction. It causes rocks at the bottom of the continental crust to become so hot that they melt. The hot molten rock, or magma, is less dense than surrounding rocks, or more buoyant, and forcefully rises as a large (kilometres wide by many kilometres deep) "blob" up through the crust. In some cases it reaches the surface forming a volcanic eruption. More commonly an intrusion forms because cool rocks near the surface of the earth cause outer portions of the blob of magma to solidify (crystallize). While the magma rises through the crust, slow cooling causes large crystals to grow but on reaching cooler rocks the outer portion of the intrusion cools quickly forming many smaller crystals. The resulting rock contains two grain sizes and is known as a porphyry. At this point an ore deposit has yet to form.

After the intrusion stops moving its interior portions are still molten and many thousands of years are required for it to crystallize. Water present in this magma becomes concentrated because minerals forming from the magma lack water in their structure. These hot-water fluids rise from depths measured in kilometres through the crystallizing magma blob and become trapped below the completely crystallized roof of the intrusion near the surface. As they rise they pick up elements such as copper, molybdenum, iron and sulphur that, like the water, are not used by minerals growing from the magma. As these fluids move upward there is less pressure on them and they begin to expand. The expanding fluids eventually become so concentrated near the top of the intrusion that they shatter the cool solidified outer rim of the intrusion. The hot fluids go rushing through the fractures but as temperature and pressure drop, dissolved elements begin to precipitate. At Brenda chalcopyrite and molybdenite along with other minerals mentioned previously were precipitated from the fluids thus filling the fractures and forming the ore body.

Plate 36: Brenda Mines Ltd. in 1990 is shown in this northwesterly view. The site is nearly all reclaimed at this time and a lake is forming in the pit. Courtesy of Brenda Mines Ltd.

Production History

Low grade mineral deposits require highly mechanized, bulk mining practices that process large amounts of ore daily at low cost per tonne. The Brenda Mine was designed for a throughput of 21,000 tonnes per day, however, the innovative and industry-first use of computer-controlled equipment and methods substantially raised this production. By 1989 a daily throughput of 31,775 tonnes was achieved at an operating cost of just $4.39 per tonne milled!

Mining operations came to an end in April 1990, as a result of an eight million tonne rock slide on the west wall of the Brenda Pit (see Plate 32). By that time 182 million tonnes of ore had been milled and 109 million tonnes of waste rock moved. Concentrates of copper minerals were shipped to Japan whereas molybdenite concentrate went to Belgium where 271,938,021 kg. of copper, 65,469 525 kg. of molybdenum, 122,814 kg. of silver and 1,777 kg. of gold were smelted (extracted) over the life of the mine. The economic benefits during the Brenda production period were $449 million in the purchase of supplies, $215 million in wages and benefits, $79 million paid in taxes and $22 million distributed as dividends to the shareholders of the company (Harris, 1992).

Mine Decommission

With mining operations finished Brenda Mines Ltd. is committed to returning the land and water to a near-natural state. Buildings have been removed, soil re-established and vegetation suitable to the local environment nurtured. The open pit will eventually fill and become a lake. At present its waters are slightly basic (pH 8) and not surprisingly contain some dissolved metals.

Water quality guidelines require that molybdenum content of mine water discharge must be less than one part per million to as low as 250 parts per billion! Brenda Mines Ltd. has commissioned several studies aimed at reducing molybdenum in the mine water and continues to work on the issue because it is probable that some of the water will eventually find its way into area streams and Okanagan Lake. As of March 1995, Brenda Mines Ltd. has committed $25 million dollars to construct and manage a water treatment plant at the mine site. When the water from the pit is discharged after treatment, it will meet drinking and irrigation water quality standards.

HIGHLAND BELL MINE

by Brian Hughes

The abandoned Highland Bell Mine is located 1.6 km east of Beaverdell on the western slope of Mount Wallace and was nationally famous for its silver production.

History

Work on the mineralized veins in the Beaverdell area date to 1889, and records indicate intermittent silver production from 1900 to 1913. Production became continuous in 1913 with the arrival of the Kettle Valley Railway.

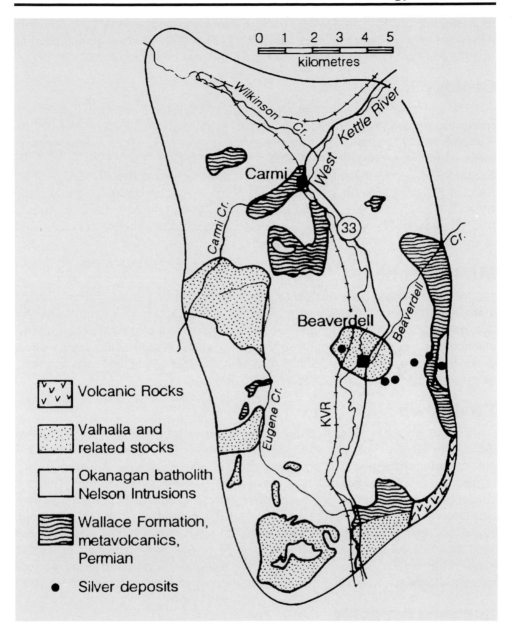

Figure 34: Geology of the Beaverdell area and location of silver deposits. Beaverdell is 80 kilometres east of Kelowna along Highway 33. Map modified from Godwin et al, 1986.

Four separate mines called the Bell, Highland Lass, Beaver, and Sally (Figure 34) produced ore until 1946 when Lietch Gold Mines Ltd. obtained control over all production under the name of Highland Bell Beaverdell Mine. Ore was sent by rail to a smelter at Trail until a 50 tonne a day concentrator was built in 1950. Afterward only concentrates were sent to Trail. Teck Corporation acquired the mine in 1970 and continued production until the mine was closed in February of 1991.

Geology

The main economic vein system of the Beaverdell mine occurs in a system of fractures in the West Kettle quartz diorite to granodiorite, part of the Nelson Batholith of Jurassic age. Thus the ore-forming processes, which involved movement of hot water solutions through a fracture system, resemble those at the Brenda Mine except that the metals in the solutions were different. Metamorphic rocks of Paleozoic and Early Mesozoic age occur as roof pendants (pieces of country rock that hang down into the granodiorite). Porphyritic quartz monzonite of the Valhalla intrusions of Jurassic to Cretaceous age intrude the Nelson rocks west of the mine.

Mineralization

Veins of quartz with smaller amounts of calcite and some fluorite formed along easterly to northeasterly trending faults and fractures. These veins also contain pyrite, galena and sphalerite, and lesser amounts of pyrrhotite, chalcopyrite, arsenopyrite, polybasite, argentite, and locally, close to fault zones, native silver wires and plates. Silver is usually associated with galena, sphalerite and antimony minerals and gold with pyrite and chalcopyrite.

Production

Due to extensive block faulting of the deposit, accurate reserves have been difficult to predict. The mill was expanded to handle 108 tonnes per day in 1954 and the mine continued at that production level until its closure. A total of 33,500 tonnes of ore were mined in a typical year (1979) and yielded 388 tonnes of lead concentrate, 399 tonnes of zinc concentrate and 97 tonnes of silver from a jig concentrate. Gross metal content of this in 1979 amounted to 4199 g of gold, 10,259,637 g of silver, 613 kg of copper, 93,324 kg of lead, 140,679 kg of zinc and 1000 kg of cadmium. Production over the life of the mine exceeded one billion grams (300 million ounces) of silver, twelve million kilograms of lead, fourteen million kilograms of zinc and significant quantities of gold, cadmium and copper.

URANIUM DEPOSITS

by Brian Hughes

During the late 1960's interest in uranium exploration was sparked by the metal's price increase to $40.00/lb and the increasing dependency of many nations on nuclear power. Of particular importance to the Kelowna area were the efforts of Power Reactor and Nuclear Fuel Development Corporation (PNC), a Japanese company. They began a search in the Kelowna area for basal uranium

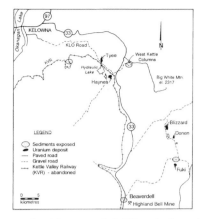

Figure 35: Uranium deposits near Kelowna.

deposits similar to those being mined in the Ningyo Toge and Tono deposits in Japan. The initial discovery of basal type uranium deposits was made at the Fuki outcrop northeast of Beaverdell (Figure 35) during a car-borne regional scintillometer survey. A scintillometer is a device that measures radioactivity given off by uranium-bearing minerals. Continued scintillometer surveys, geochemistry studies of soils, stream silts and groundwater, regional mapping and widespread drilling led to the discovery of another deposit by PNC geologists, the Tyee just north of Hydraulic Lakes. As other exploration groups became involved deposits were found at Haynes Lake and, the largest deposit, the Blizzard property. The Blizzard deposit has reported reserves of over 2.1 million tonnes grading 0.226% uranium. However, in 1970 the British Columbia government imposed a moratorium on all uranium exploration and mining and to date all of these deposits remain undeveloped.

Regional Geology

The regional geologic setting in this portion of the Okanagan Highland consists of the uplifted Shuswap metamorphic rocks intruded by the Valhalla granitic rocks of Mesozoic age (Figure 34). Further intrusion took place during the Tertiary represented by the Coryell intrusions composed of monzonite and syenite. During the Pliocene large north-south trending streams developed on the surface of these rocks and widespread sand and gravel deposits including carbonaceous material (organic remains of plants) were laid down. These sediments were later overlain by plateau basalts of late Tertiary age (see Chapters Two, Three and Four).

Origin of the Uranium Deposits

The mineralization was likely derived from the Valhalla and Coryell intrusive rocks that are known to have a high background Uranium content. Uranium mineralization was deposited in the more carbonaceous parts of the river sediments that were mantled with basaltic lava flows (Figure 36).

It is believed that groundwater percolating through the uranium-bearing intrusive rocks dissolved the uranium and carried it downward in solution. When the flow path of these solutions intersected carbonaceous parts of the sediments, reducing conditions were encountered which caused the precipitation of the uranium minerals. Mineralization varies between deposits and includes uranium oxides and phosphates such as saleeite, ningyoite and autinite. Other minerals associated with these deposits are iron sulfides and oxides such as pyrite, marca-

ORIGIN OF THE HYDRAULIC LAKE URANIUM DEPOSIT

Stage 1: Late Tertiary Paleostream Episode

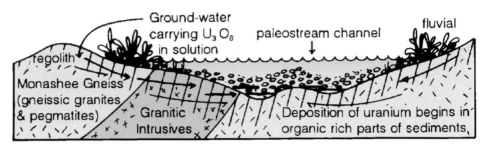

Stage 2: Plateau Volcanic Episode

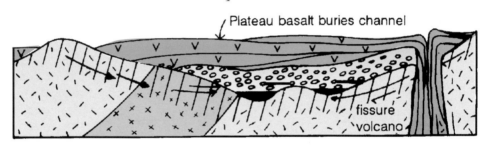

Present Day

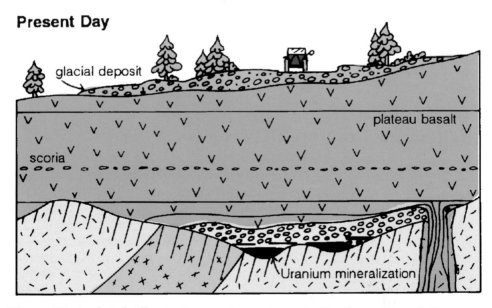

Figure 36: A sketch illustrating various stages in the formation of the uranium deposits near Kelowna.

site and hematite. Most mineralization is observed as coatings on sediment grains and as a partial cement in the matrix of the sand and gravel sediments.

Continued uplift of the Okanagan Highland terminated this uranium enrichment process. Where later glacial erosion was not too deep, these basal type uranium deposits were preserved below protective caps of plateau basalts.

A typical basal type environment of stream troughs in weathered pre-Tertiary rocks filled with clastic sediments and overlain by plateau basaltic rocks can be seen in cross-section in several road outcrops in the area. One of the best sections can be viewed on the Okanagan Falls logging road approximately 2.5 kilometres south of its junction with the Big White access road east of Highway 33 (Figure 35). At this location several basaltic flows displaying columnar structure (referred to as the West Kettle Columns) are exposed and overlie sand and gravel beds of Tertiary age which in turn overlie weathered and leached pre-Tertiary intrusive rocks. Also, several sections of the same type can be viewed on the Kettle Valley Railway between KLO Creek and Bellevue Creek trestles. The only section with significant uranium mineralization that can be seen is the Fuki showing near Deer Creek located at Kilometre 22.8 on the Beaver Creek forestry road east of Beaverdell.

Reported Ore Reserves

Drilling has indicated that the uranium deposits are commonly channel shaped varying in width from less than 10 metres to over 100 metres, and ranging from less than a metre thick to over 40 metres in the case of the higher grade Blizzard deposit.

Deposit	Tonnes of Ore	Grade	Tonnes of U
Blizzard	2.2 million	0.183%	4020
Tyee	2.1 million	0.031%	650
Donen	1.0 million	0.040%	400
Fuki	0.5 million	0.025%	125
Haynes Lake	2.0 million	0.017%	340
North Tyee	1.0 million	0.017%	170

Significance of the Uranium Deposits

The discovery and development potential of these uranium deposits triggered a strong environmental opposition in the Okanagan region. This opposition forced the British Columbia government in 1970 to retro-actively terminate all uranium exploration in the province. Companies have never been compensated for their exploration costs.

Apart from demonstrating the effectiveness of environmental lobbyists and in contrast the ineffectiveness of the exploration industry to present defensible counter-arguments, there is an economic significance to this. The total gross value of uranium ore in the deposits exceeds 125 million U.S. dollars in 1995. The loss of this has to be weighed against other cost-benefit factors some of global impact magnitude such as the possible abuse of radioactive materials. It also has to be measured against the successful uranium mining industry that has helped sustain the provinces of Saskatchewan and Ontario for many years. One fact is sure, it sends the message out to the world mineral industry that British Columbia can be a tough place to do business.

AGGREGATES

Aggregate refers to sand, gravel and rock deposits used for construction purposes. The majority is used for the manufacture of concrete and pavement. It is a substantial industry which accounts for 5% of the total mineral production of British Columbia.

Most of the sand and gravel deposits that are presently developed in the Okanagan consist of glaciofluvial deposits formed when the Fraser glacier melted. A major meltwater channel is located on the west side of the lake, another in the vicinity of the airport, and another along the East Kelowna Escarpment. Parts of these deposits have been mined for sand and gravel, but many extensions of this valuable resource now lie beneath housing developments (for example, Crawford Estates in the Mission) or are in the Agricultural Land Reserve. For aggregate producers in the Okanagan, there are no other nearby deposits, and the industry locally is facing a crisis while the public is forced to pay increased costs as deposits further away are utilized. This is a province-wide phenomenon that is just now receiving a little attention.

CHAPTER 12

HYDROLOGY AND WATERSHED MANAGEMENT

by Don Dobson

Hydrologically Kelowna is situated in the Okanagan Lake Watershed (Figure 37). A watershed is defined as the land area that accumulates all the runoff (surface and groundwater) above a specified point. The southern boundary of the watershed is the outlet of the lake located at Penticton, and the northern boundary is just north of Armstrong.

The entire watershed for Okanagan Lake has an area of 6,187 square kilometres. The City of Kelowna encompasses the lower areas of several streams that flow into Okanagan Lake. Mission Creek is the largest tributary in the Okanagan Lake watershed, and has an area of 900 square kilometres. It accounts for 15% of the entire watershed. The other main streams in the Kelowna area are: McDougall Creek, Powers Creek, Trepanier Creek, Lambly (Bear) Creek, Kelowna(Mill) Creek, Bellevue Creek, Brandt Creek and Lebanon Creek.

Water Source

The Okanagan Valley is part of the Interior Dry Belt. Annual precipitation over the Okanagan Basin averages approximately 554 mm, the majority of which falls as snow. Although precipitation for the period June - October averages 237 mm, most of it evaporates before it can runoff. Unless water from the melting snow is stored for use during the dry summer months, there would be insufficient water in the streams to meet domestic and irrigation demands. When snow is the primary source of water to a stream, approximately 90% of the annual runoff volume occurs during the period May-July when the snow is melting (Figure 38).

Water Cycle

By reviewing the normal consumption of the water cycle for the Okanagan Basin (Figure 39), it becomes evident how little water there really is available. Of the 554 mm of precipitation that falls in the basin, 419 mm is used by the forests and other vegetation for evapotranspiration including infiltration to groundwater,

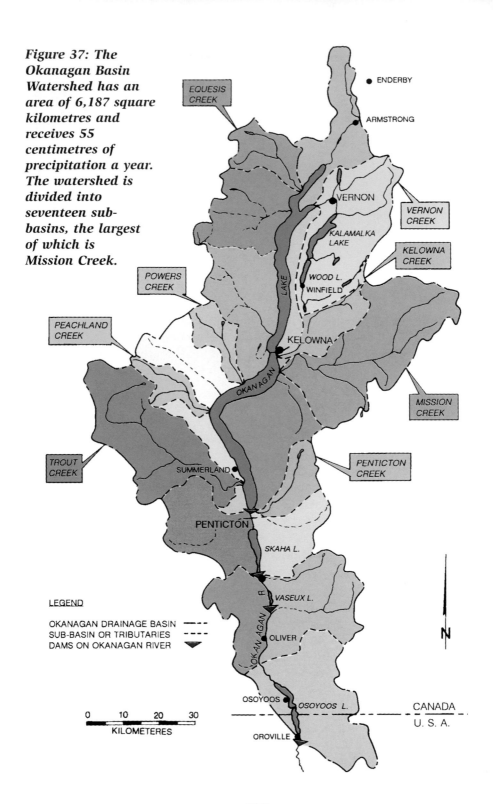

Figure 37: The Okanagan Basin Watershed has an area of 6,187 square kilometres and receives 55 centimetres of precipitation a year. The watershed is divided into seventeen sub-basins, the largest of which is Mission Creek.

EQUESIS CREEK

ENDERBY

ARMSTRONG

VERNON

VERNON CREEK

KALAMALKA LAKE

KELOWNA CREEK

POWERS CREEK

WOOD L.
WINFIELD

PEACHLAND CREEK

LAKE

KELOWNA

MISSION CREEK

OKANAGAN

TROUT CREEK

SUMMERLAND

PENTICTON CREEK

PENTICTON

SKAHA L.

LEGEND

OKANAGAN DRAINAGE BASIN — — —
SUB-BASIN OR TRIBUTARIES — — —
DAMS ON OKANAGAN RIVER ▼

VASEUX L.

OKANAGAN R.

OLIVER

N

0   10   20   30
KILOMETERES

OSOYOOS

OSOYOOS L.

CANADA
U.S.A.

OROVILLE

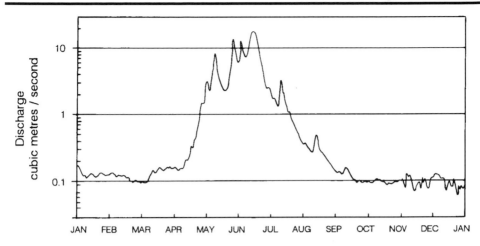

Figure 38: A typical hydrograph of a stream such as Mission Creek in the Interior of British Columbia.

122 mm flows into Okanagan Lake of which 53 mm evaporates. This leaves only 13 mm (2%) of the surface water to be used for domestic or irrigation purposes.

Water Use

Water required to meet the daily needs of the City of Kelowna is obtained either from Okanagan Lake or from several of the local creeks. Black Mountain Irrigation District has water licenses in the Mission Creek watershed with reservoirs (Ideal Lake, Fish Hawk Lake, Graystoke Lake, Mission Lake) located in the uplands that store 15.4 million cubic metres. Southeast Kelowna Irrigation District has water licenses in the Hydraulic Creek watershed with reservoirs (Hydraulic

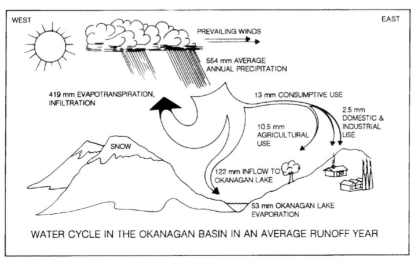

Figure 39: The Water Cycle in the Okanagan Basin

Lake, Browne Lake, Turtle Lake) that store 16.3 million cubic metres. Glenmore-Ellison Irrigation District has the rights to store 6.9 million cubic metres of water in reservoirs (Postill Lake, Bulman Lake, South Lake) in the Kelowna Creek watershed. Another major supplier is Rutland Waterworks which uses groundwater as the source of water for its users in the Rutland area (refer to Chapter 13 for additional information on groundwater).

Management

Surface water is managed by the Water Management Branch of BC Environment. Water may be used from a stream or lake only after a water license is issued from the government. The reservoirs in most cases are pre-existing lakes where the volume of water that could be stored was increased by the construction of a dam at the outlet, with control works to regulate the amount of water released. Typically, water is stored in the reservoir as the snow melts during May and June, until the reservoir is full. Water is then released according to the needs for domestic and irrigation uses over the July - October period. Depending upon the system, irrigation can utilize up to 80% of the water supplied by a water district. In a dry year nearly all the water in storage will be used by the end of October.

Multiple Use Watersheds

Land in the watersheds is managed for multiple uses. Most of the uplands of the watersheds are Crown land, meaning that the land is owned by the province. The lowlands or valley bottom lands are all private land. The multiple use philosophy provides for a wide variety of uses on private land, ranging from agriculture to industrial and residential developments. On Crown land the licensed uses include cattle grazing, forest development, mineral development, water resource development, guiding and trapping. Another important but not licensed use is recreation.

Effect of Modern Land Use

Land use practices can have significant impacts on the quality and quantity of the water that runs off the land. Timber harvesting is the dominant activity on Crown land, where the majority of the runoff is derived. Forest development is carried out by timber companies such as Riverside Forest Products Ltd., Weyerhaeuser Canada Ltd. and Gorman Bros. Lumber Ltd. in accordance with policies of the Ministry of Forests. Tree species range from Interior Douglas fir and Ponderosa pine which occur on the lower slopes above the valley floor, to Lodgepole pine, spruce, and larch which dominate the upland. Most harvesting over the past two decades has occurred on the upland and focused on the Lodgepole pine stands which have been infested with mountain pine beetle.

Water Quantity

Logging can affect the hydrology of the watershed by changing the quantity and timing of runoff. As the forest cover is removed more snow accumulates on the ground. Up to 30% more water can occur in the form of snow in a clear-cut opening compared to that in an undisturbed forest. This increase in water becomes significant when the amount of forest cover removed exceeds 20% of the watershed area. It has also been determined, through research, that snow in the clear-cut openings melts approximately two weeks earlier than in the natural forest.

Water Quality

Water quality can also be affected by forest development activities. Soil disturbance from roads, landings and skid trails can increase the amount of sediment that reaches a stream. However, this impact can be controlled through careful construction and maintenance procedures. The water quality may also be affected by increased runoff volumes in the streams resulting from removal of the forest cover and erosion in the stream channel. This impact can be controlled also by planning the rate at which the forest cover is removed so as to maintain close to natural flows in the stream.

Vital Resource

All of the watersheds within the Okanagan basin, including those in the Kelowna area, are vital to the environmental sustainability of the basin. Through increased awareness of the impacts of human activities in the watersheds and knowing that for every action there is a reaction, the environmental quality can be protected. Whether it is the intense development on the valley floor within the City of Kelowna, or activities on Crown land, the priority should always be to protect the water resource.

Summary

It is important to be aware that only 25% of the total water that falls on the basin appears as runoff, and of that amount only 15% is available for human uses. Since water has always been a scarce resource in the Okanagan Valley, it should be managed with care. With populations continuing to increase, the demand for clean water will also increase. Based on the fact that the amount of available water is limited, optimal management of the resource will be essential. To accomplish this will require additional planning on a watershed basis. Detailed watershed management plans will be required that incorporate forest management on Crown land and urban water management on private land. Management in isolation, that is, Crown land managed separately from private land, and vice versa cannot continue. Water is the life blood of this valley.

CHAPTER 13

GROUNDWATER RESOURCES

Groundwater refers to free water that occurs below the surface of the Earth. Its upper surface is referred to as the water table. All lakes, ponds and stream levels more or less define this level. All groundwater originates from precipitation in the form of rain or snow (Figure 39). Some water is evaporated, some is used by plants and trees, some runs off into streams, rivers and lakes, and some is retained by soils. Whatever remains, usually less than 5%, sinks into the ground and becomes groundwater. Fractures in rocks and pores between sedimentary sand, gravel, silt and clay particles serve to store groundwater and permit its slow movement. Such subsurface materials or deposits that can store and transmit groundwater are referred to as aquifers, and holes drilled into the aquifer that produce groundwater economically are called water wells.

Groundwater Flow

The flow of water through an aquifer is controlled by two factors: (1) The ability of the subsurface soil or rock to transmit water, known as hydraulic conductivity, and (2) the slope of the water table which is called the hydraulic gradient. Aquifers collect water in recharge areas which are at high elevation. The amount of recharge possible is related to the infiltration capacity of the surface. For example, more water would seep into a gravel deposit than a clay deposit.

Everyone knows that water flows from high spots to low spots. Thus, groundwater enters in recharge zones at high elevation and flows through one or more aquifers to a lower elevation. Where the land surface is intersected natural springs may occur forming a discharge zone.

Environmental Sensitivity

The location and characteristics of groundwater recharge and discharge zones in watersheds place constraints on land use and development. For example, pollutants allowed to enter a recharge zone, perhaps at a landfill site, may lead to contamination of the entire "downstream" portion of the aquifer. Surface changes in a recharge zone can affect the quantity of water entering the subsurface. For example, removal of forest cover by fire or logging increases the amount of groundwater whereas urbanization and paved surfaces decreases the amount of groundwater. This in turn may have an important impact on discharge zones at lower elevations. Landslides often originate in groundwater discharge zones where springs and high pore pressure reduce the strength of soils on a slope.

Groundwater Use in the Kelowna Area

There are thousands of water wells in the Kelowna area, but unfortunately a comprehensive study of the various aquifers that exist is not available. Historically, groundwater has always been a major component of the city's domestic and agricultural water supply.

Magnitude of Groundwater Use

The magnitude of groundwater use is illustrated by the Rutland Waterworks District installations. Just below the Rutland fan in the vicinity of Mission Creek, the Rutland Waterworks District has developed 15 wells between 32 and 106 metres in depth that serve 4,500 connections (1991) in the Rutland District. The aquifer is called the Rutland Aquifer (Figure 40) and the wells are pumped at rates of 900 to 5,600 litres per minute. Average monthly summer production is 681 million litres, with consumption dropping to 205 million litres in winter (courtesy of Rutland Water District). Total production in 1977 was three billion litres (800,000,000 U.S.gallons), in 1991 it was three and a half billion litres and in 1994 four and a quarter billion litres.

In comparison, the Black Mountain Irrigation District in 1994 withdrew a total of 125 billion litres from Mission Creek, nearly 30 times the quantity withdrawn from the Rutland aquifer. East Kelowna Irrigation District withdraws similar amounts from a tributary to Mission Creek.

Many water districts in the Okanagan Valley supplement surface water resources with groundwater. All of the rural developments including some subdivisions and some orchards in the area rely on water wells. Numerous golf courses have drilled their own water wells for maintenance of their fairways. Several bottled water factories, at least one brewery, several dairy product factories, and all major cattle ranches in the region rely on groundwater resources.

Geology of the Rutland Aquifer

A cross-section through the Rutland aquifer is shown in Figure 40. It occurs as an extensive gravel bed 100 metres thick that is overlain by outwash deposits and till inferred to belong to the Fraser glaciation, silt and clay deposits of Lake Penticton, and fluvial-deltaic deposits which have accumulated since the end of glacial time in the former embayment of Okanagan Lake now occupied by Kelowna.

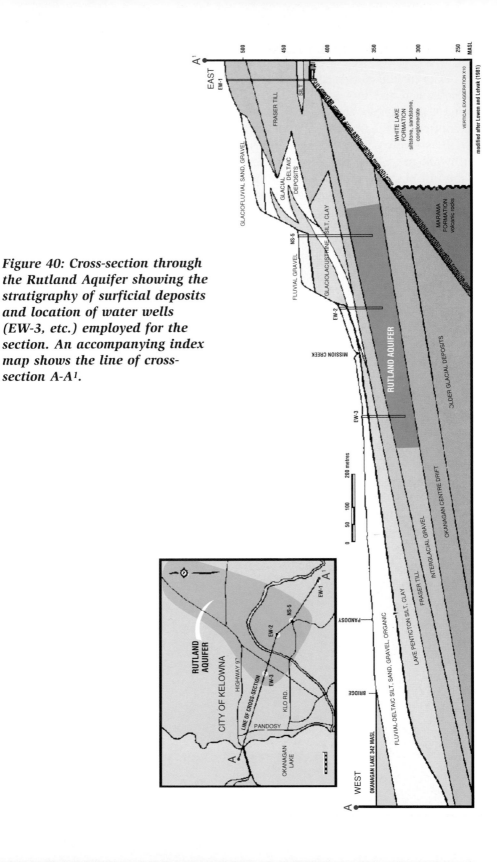

Figure 40: Cross-section through the Rutland Aquifer showing the stratigraphy of surficial deposits and location of water wells (EW-3, etc.) employed for the section. An accompanying index map shows the line of cross-section A-A¹.

Data for the construction of this cross-section have been derived from water wells (Lowen and Letvak, 1981), a surficial geology map (Nasmith, 1962), and from 1994 drill hole data at the east end of the floating bridge (supplied through the courtesy of the Ministry of Transportation and Highways).

It is known from regional information that the Rutland aquifer extends northward to at least the airport although the water within it is not of uniform quality. In places it is high in iron and manganese. Remarkably, the water from the aquifer appears to have remained unaffected by agricultural chemicals and residential septic systems in East Kelowna.

How and where this aquifer is recharged is not known at this time. It is possible that a thick gravel exposed in Gallagher's Canyon (Plate 20) is part of the aquifer. The base of this outcrop is at an elevation of approximately 420 metres and correlates with a projection of the aquifer's stratigraphic position in the subsurface. If this is the case, then a downstream section of Mission Creek flows directly over the aquifer. It is possible therefore that this portion of the creek may be one of the main points of recharge for this important aquifer.

Groundwater Research

Although groundwater was included in early studies of the Okanagan Basin Water Authority, the scope of this work was far short of the kind of information that is now, over twenty years later, critically required. For example, pumping too much water from an aquifer could cause subsidence of the surface. As learned earlier this century in Mexico City, this can affect buildings and may impact on base levels of streams. Modifying surface water discharge changes natural flow, stream regime, and may have important long range impacts on biologic systems. For example, it can affect fish spawning habitat conditions. Although flows are now regulated insuring a certain flow at all times in Mission Creek, the benefits and affects of this have never been scientifically assessed. There could be an existing or a potential problem here for currently utilized groundwater and surface water in Mission Creek watershed in the Kelowna area.

CHAPTER 14

EARTH SCIENCE AND THE FUTURE OF THE OKANAGAN VALLEY

The growth and application of earth science in the twentieth century has been explosive, but the importance of these developments have yet to be appreciated, especially by local governments in British Columbia. Geology affects every aspect of modern life in the Okanagan. The best agricultural land is developed on a variety of surficial deposits which reflect their geologic origin. Possibly, the Okanagan's unique soils are responsible for the success of grape growing and a thriving wine industry. Mines and mineral development have had a major economic impact and allowed the development of advanced innovative techniques in mining engineering that are now in demand on a world wide scale.

The beauty and variety of the Okanagan terrain is widely known and due to a complex and awesome geologic history. This geologic design work of Mother Nature continues to attract more and more visitors, sustain a diversified tourist industry, and make the Okanagan a preferred place to live and enjoy almost every type of recreational pursuit. However, entering the twenty-first century, the resources of the Okanagan will have to be known and understood in far more detail than at present. Water management including the preservation and enhancement of existing water quality will be the most challenging task. Far too little is being done about water use issues at this time. This resource is limited and must be managed in optimum harmony with an array of conflicting land use issues, not the least of which is the preservation of natural biological systems. The Kokanee, wildlife, forest, and many of our basic needs all depend on wise and appropriate water management.

Watershed Management

Serious watershed management is now a government mandate in British Columbia as set out in the new Forest Practice Code. The forest industry in the Okanagan is responding swiftly and effectively to this new mandate, and although adjustments in harvesting techniques will take time, the long term prospect for greatly improved watershed management, better water quality, and healthier forests can be envisaged. However, management of both Crown and private land has to be integrated.

Requirements for earth science, hydrology and engineering expertise in the forest industry and water management has experienced a surging demand, and is now straining available scientific personnel. This demand will increase and extend into the future which bodes well for the young scientists of the province.

Construction Materials

It has been shown that modern geotechnical engineering can be applied to build larger and higher structures in the Okanagan. The highway system is gradually being improved, large rural and suburban developments are under construction, major industries are emerging, and many construction materials are required. All of this activity involves concrete and pavement, products of the aggregate industry, and in turn the existence of accessible aggregate resources. At the rate sand and gravel deposits of both fluvial and glacial origin are being used for building sites, the Okanagan will soon be depleted of this valuable resource, yet there appears to be little awareness or concern for this.

Residential Development

Residential development in the future is projected to depend on major capital expenditures for sewage treatment. Although controversial, development using individual septic systems in thick suitable surficial deposits where terrain is well drained can be an economical and environmentally safe option. Through modern geologic and hydrogeologic studies, it is feasible to locate terrain that is ideally suited for individual sewage systems without jeopardizing the environment. Failure of septic systems is rooted in poor evaluation and siting techniques and construction methods of the past. There are more data supporting the use of tiles fields with attendant environmental integrity than not, a good example of this is the Rutland aquifer and how it has remained uncontaminated throughout the years.

Urban and Regional Planning

Urban and regional planners are beginning to respond to some concerns regarding storm water management, hazard land evaluation, and flooding, but a suitable and detailed terrain and hydrologic data base for evaluation of these is lacking in the Okanagan. Compared to other places in the world, even in Canada, our almost nonexistent database for these important terrain characteristics is insufficient and obscure. There has to be a long term commitment to improve.

Mineral Resources

Minerals such as gold, silver, lead, zinc, copper and molybdenum still lie undetected in the bedrock of the Okanagan landscape. According to recent work and new theories involving plate tectonics, the diversified bedrock terrain west of

Okanagan Lake offers the best prospects for new discoveries. Volcanic deposits of the Kelowna caldera complex also offer possibilities for rare minerals such as opal and agate, but little exploration has been conducted. The impetus for encouraging mineral exploration lies with government, and a good start would be comprehensive and detailed bedrock and surficial geology maps of the Okanagan Valley.

Summary

If a conclusion to this book can be written, it has to be that there are substantial opportunities unprecedented in history for students of earth science in the growth and well being of the Okanagan. Politicians who are aware of our critical resource needs can play a leading role in channeling sufficient funds to enhance the resource data base. The academic community should be encouraged to expand teaching and research in earth science and engineering. A central well stocked science library is critically required, and outlets for remote sensing products and government science publications are necessities. Geotechnical engineering professionals should begin to inventory soils and drilling data and related research to help build a resource data base for public use. Residents have a role to play in learning to appreciate the usefulness and/or sensitivity of the resources and be reasonably tolerant in land use conflicts. Planners have to learn more about how to economically utilize the fruits of earth science in a socially agreeable, environmentally acceptable and economy-sustaining manner. There is much to be done. Above all, get outside and enjoy this beautiful part of British Columbia!

References

Agriculture Canada, 1993. Soil Landscapes of Canada, British Columbia-South. Canada Soil Inventory, Centre for Land and Biological Resources Research, Agriculture Canada, Contribution Number 89-03.

Alley, N.F., 1976. The Palynology and Paleoclimatic Significance of a Dated Core of Holocene Peat, Okanagan Valley, Southern British Columbia. Can. J. Earth Sci., v.13, p.1131-1144.

Bailey, J. and Rousseau, M.K., 1994. An Archaeological Assessment of Prehistoric Site DKQw 36 in Okanagan Mountain Park, Near Naramata, South-Central B.C. Report on file at the Archaeology Branch. Victoria, B.C.

Baker, J. (Ed), 1975. Okanagan College Archaeological Research Project, Okanagan College, Kelowna.

Baker, J., 1990. Archaeological Research Concerning the Origins of the Okanagan People. In Okanagan Sources. Ed. Jean Webber. Penticton, B.C. Theytus Books Ltd.

Borden, C.E., 1979. Peopling and Early Cultures of the Pacific Northwest: A View from British Columbia, Canada. Science 203:1963-971.

Buchannan, R.G., and Haughton, D.R., 1978. Physical, Chemical, Mineralogical Properties of B.C. Glaciolacustrine Silts and Fundamental Design Implications. Ministry of Transportation and Highways, Victoria, B.C.

Cairnes, C.E., 1932. Mineral Resources of Northern Okanagan Valley, British Columbia. Geol. Surv. Canada, Summary Report 1931, Part A, p. 66-109.

Cairnes,C.E., 1937. Mineral Deposits of the West Half of Kettle River Area, British Columbia. Geol. Surv. Canada, Paper 37-21.

Carr, J.M., 1967. Geology of the Brenda Lake Area. B.C. Minister of Mines and Petroleum Resources, Ann. Rept., 1967, p. 183-212.

Cass, D.E., Kenning, B.F.I., and Rawlings, G., 1992. The Philpott Road Debris Failure-Kelowna, B.C. 1990: The Impacts of Geology, Hydrology and Logging Activities. Geotechnique and Natural Hazards; a Symposium sponsored by the Vancouver Geotechnical Society and the Canadian Geotechnical Society, May 6-9, 1992, p. 319-325.

Chatwin, S.C., Howes, D.E., Schwab, J.W., and Swanston, D.N., 1994. A Guide for Management of Landslide-Prone Terrain in the Pacific Northwest, Second Edition. Research Program, Ministry of Forests, British Columbia, 220p.

Christopher, P.A., 1977. Uranium Mineralization in the Hydraulic Lake Area, British Columbia; in Geological Fieldwork 1976. B.C. Dept. Mines and Petrol. Resources, p.11-14.

Church, B.N., 1980a. Geology of the Kelowna Tertiary Outlier (West Half) (NTS 82E). B.C. Min. Energy, Mines and Petrol. Resources, Preliminary Map 39.

Church, B.N., 1981b. Geology of the Kelowna Tertiary Outlier (East Half) (NTS 82E). B.C. Min. Energy, Mines and Petrol. Resources, Preliminary Map 45.

Cole, D., and Lockner, B., 1989. The Journals of George M. Dawson, British Columbia, 1875-1878. v.I, 1875-1876, 296p.; v.II, 1877-1878, 297-611p. University of British Columbia Press.

Copp, S., 1980. A Dated Pictograph from the South Okanagan Valley of British Columbia. Canadian Rock Art Research Associates Newsletter 14:44-48.

Corner, J., 1968. Pictographs: Indian Rock Paintings, Vernon, B.C.

Dawson, G.M., 1878. Explorations in British Columbia. Geol. Surv. Canada, Report of Progress 1876-77, p. 16-149.

Dawson, G.M., 1879. Report on Exploration in the Southern Portion of British Columbia. Geol. Survey Can., Report of Progress 1877-1878, Pt. B, p. 157-158.

Dawson, G.M., 1879. Preliminary Report on the Physical and Geological Features of the Interior of British Columbia. Geol. Surv. Canada, Report of Progress, p. 1877-78.

Downing, P.B., 1993. Okanagan Opal. Lapidary Journal, v.16, no.11, p.63-66.

Evans, J., 1993. The Okanagan Lake Bridge. Kelowna Centennial Museum Association, Kelowna, B.C. V1Y 6S7, 11 p.

Evans, S.G., 1982. Landslides and Surficial Deposits in Urban Areas of British Columbia: A Review. Can. Geotech. Jour., v. 19, no. 3, p. 269-288.

Eyles, N., Mullins, H.T., and Hine, A.C., 1990. Thick and Fast: Sedimentation in a Pleistocene Fiord Lake of British Columbia, Canada. Geology, v.18, p. 1153-1157.

Fairbank, B.D., and Faulkner, R.L., 1992. Geothermal Resources of British Columbia. Geol. Surv. Canada, Open File 2526, Map, Scale 1:2,000,000.

Falk, L., 1982. Hiking Trails in the Okanagan. Mosaic Enterprises, 1420 St Paul Street, Kelowna, British Columbia, 60p.

Fladmark, K.R., 1983. Times and Places: Environmental Correlates of Mid-to-Late

Wisconsinan Human Population Expansion in North Amercia. *In* Early Man in the New World. Beverly Hill, California. Sage Publications.

Fladmark, K.R., Driver, J.C., and Alexander, D., 1988. The Paleoindian Component at Charlie Lake Cave (HbRf 39) British Columbia. American Antiquity v.53:371-384.

Flint, R.F., 1935. "White Silt" Deposits in the Okanagan Valley, British Columbia. Roy. Soc. Can. Trans., v.29, p.107-114.

Flint, R.F., 1935. Glacial Features of the Southern Okanagan. Geol. Soc. Amer. Bull., v.46, p.169-193.

Fulton, R.J., 1965. Silt Deposition in Late-Glacial Lakes in Southern British Columbia. Am. Jour. Sci., v.263, p.553-570.

Fulton, R.J., 1969. Glacial Lake History, Southern Interior Plateau, British Columbia. Geol. Surv. Canada, Paper 69-37, 14 p.

Fulton, R.J.and G.W.Smith, 1978. Late Pleistocene Stratigraphy of South-Central British Columbia. Can. Jour. Earth Sci., v.15, p.971-980.

Fulton, R.J., Irving, E., and Wheadon, P.M., 1992. Stratigraphy and Paleomagnetism of Brunhes and Matuyama (> 790 ka) Quaternary Deposits at Merritt, British Columbia. Can. Jour. Earth Sci., v.29, no.1, p.76-92.

Godwin, C.I., Watson, P.H., and Shen, K., 1986. Genesis of the Lass Vein System, Beaverdell Silver Camp, South-central British Columbia. Can. Jour. Earth Sci., v.23, p. 1615-1626.

Harris, G.R.,1992. Mine Closure - Brenda Mines Ltd. (paper delivered to the Mining Association of Canada).

Hickson, C.J., 1992. Volcanism in the Canadian Cordillera: Should We Worry?. Geotechnique and Natural Hazards. BiTech Publishers Ltd., Vancouver, B.C., p. 31-40.

Holland, S.S., 1964. Landforms of British Columbia, a Physiographic Outline. B.C. Dept. Mines and Pet. Res., Bull. 48, p.138.

Howie, J.A., and Jinks, A.R., 1994. The Grand Okanagan Lake Front Resort and Conference Centre, Kelowna, B.C.. 47th Canadian Geotechnical Conference, 1994, Halifax, N.S., p. 200-209.

Hudson, D.R., 1990. The Okanagan Indians of British Columbia. In Okanagan Sources. Ed. Jean Webber. Penticton, B.C. Theytus Books Ltd.

Keyser, J.D., 1992. Indian Rock Art of the Columbia Plateau. University of Washington Press. Seattle.

Little, H.W., 1961. Kettle River, West Half, British Columbia. Geol. Surv. Canada,

Map 15-1961.

Lowen, D.A. and Letvak, D.B., 1981. Report on Groundwater-Surface Water Interrelationship, Lower Mission Creek, B.C.. B.C. Min. Envir., Water Management Branch, Victoria, B.C., 19p.

Lundy, A. (dePfyffer), and Zoellner, D. (Whitham), 1990. Tours Made Easy. RR#4, 4881 Lakeshore Road, Kelowna, B.C. V1Y 7R3, 102 p.

Macauley, H.A., Hobson, G.D., and Fulton, R.J., 1972. Bedrock Topography of the North Okanagan Valley and Stratigraphy of the Unconsolidated Fill. Geol. Surv. Canada, Paper 72-8, 17p.

Malcolm, G., 1995. New Life for Brenda Mines. Mining Magazine, London, England, p.217-219

Mathews, W.H., 1944. Glacial Lakes and Ice Retreat in South Central British Columbia. Roy. Soc. Canada Trans., v.38, sec. 4, p. 39-57.

Mathews, W.M., 1988. Neogene Geology of the Okanagan Highland, British Columbia. Can Jour. Earth Sci., v. 25, no. 5, p. 725-731.

Meyers, R.E. and Taylor, W.A., 1989. Lode Gold-Silver Occurrences of the Okanagan Region, South-Central British Columbia (82E/W, 82L/SW). B.C Min. Energy, Mines and Petrol. Res., Geol. Surv. Br., O.F. 1989-5.

Ministry of Forests, 1990. Investigation into the Causes of the Destructive Debris Flow, Joe Rich-Belgo Creek Area, June 12, 1990. B.C. Min. Forests, Forest Service Investigation Team, Penticton Forest District, 57p.

Nasmith, H., 1981. Late Glacial History and Surficial Deposits of the Okanagan Valley, British Columbia. B.C. Min. Energy, Mines and Petrol. Res., Bull. 46, 46p.

Nyland, D., and Miller, G.E., 1977. Geologic Hazards and Urban Development of Silt Deposits in the Penticton Area. B.C. Ministry of Highways and Public Works, Geotechnical Materials Branch.

Okulitch, A.V., 1979. Geology and Mineral Occurrences of the Thompson-Shuswap-Okanagan Region, South-Central British Columbia. Geol. Surv. Canada, O.F. 637.

Paynter, S., 1991. First Time Around. Published by the author, Box 166, Westbank, B.C. V0H 2A0, 136 p.

Pegusch, W., 1957. The Kelowna Floating Bridge. Eng. Jour., April, 1957, p. 413-421.

Peto, P.(1973) Petrochemical Study of the Similkameen Batholith, British Columbia: Geol. Soc. Amer. Bull. v.84, p.3977-84.

Reinecke, L., 1915. Physiography of the Beaverdell Map-Area and the Southern Part of the Interior Plateau of British Columbia. Geol. Surv. Canada, Mus., Bull. no.11.

Rice, H.M.A., 1960. Geology and Mineral Deposits of the Princeton Map Area, B.C. Geol. Survey, Mem. 243, 136 p.

Richards, T.H. and Rousseau, M.K., 1987. Late Prehistoric Cultural Horizons on the Canadian Plateau. Simon Fraser University, Department of Archaeology Publication 16, Burnaby, B.C.

Roed, M.A., 1991. Scenic Canyon Regional Park: Natural History Unfolds Here. Okanagan Life, Summer, 1991, p.11 and 18.

Ryder, J.M., and Thompson, B., 1986. Neoglaciation in the Southern Coast Mountains of British Columbia: Chronology Prior to the Late Neoglacial Maximum. Can. Jour. Earth Sc., v.23, no. 3., p.273-287.

Sanford, B., 1978. McCulloch's Wonder, The Story of the Kettle Valley Railway. Whitecap Books, Vancouver, British Columbia, 260 p.

Soregaroli, A.E., and Whitford, D.F., 1974. Brenda. CIM Special Volume No. 15, Part B, p. 186-194.

Shaw, J. and Archer, J., 1979. Deglaciation and Glaciolacustrine Conditions, Okanagan Valley, British Columbia, Canada in Moraines and Varves(INQUA Symposium), Rotterdam, A.A.Balkema, p.347-355.

Shewchuk, M., 1992. Okanagan Country, An Outdoor Recreation Guide. Sonotek Publishing Ltd., P.O.Box 1752, Merritt, B.C. V0K 2B0, 176p.

Smith, K., 1990. The West Wall Failure at Brenda Mines. Brenda Mines Ltd..

Tempelman-Kluit, D. J., 1989. Geological Map with Mineral Occurrences, Fossil Localities, Radiometric Ages and Gravity Field for Penticton Map Area (NTS 82E), Southern British Columbia. Geol. Surv. Canada, O.F. 1969.

Tempelman-Kluit, D. and Harakal, J.E., 1986. Extension Across the Eocene Okanagan Crustal Shear in Southern British Columbia. Geology, v. 14, p. 318-321.

Turner, N., Bouchard, R., and Kennedy, D., 1980. Ethnobotany of the Okanagan-Colville Indians of British Columbia and Washington. British Columbia Provincial Museum Occasional Papers Series, No. 21.

Wilson, R.L. and Carlson, C., 1980. The Archaeology of Kamloops. Simon Fraser University, Department of Archaeology Publication 7, Burnaby, B.C.

Wittneben, U., 1986. Soils of the Okanagan and Similkameen Valleys. BC Ministry of Environment, Report No. 52, B.C. Soil Survey, 229 p.

APPENDIX A

A SIGHTSEER'S DELIGHT

The following field trip includes driving directions for a day long trip (100 kilometres) through the Kelowna area focusing on major geologic and landscape features. Reference is made to Chapter Eight, Geologic Landmarks of the Kelowna Area where the features are described in more detail. Each feature is numbered (parenthesis) and located on a map (Figure 19) which should be kept handy as the tour progresses.

Start at Knox Mountain (1):

Drive to the top of the mountain by following Ellis Street; look at banded and varved silts of glacial Lake Penticton on way up (2); park in the parking lot and take the trail to the gazebo view point. Refer to rosette directional map in Figure 20.

To Mount Dilworth Drivepast (3):

Go down Ellis, turn left at Clement Avenue, then right at Gordon Drive (site of landslide, all landscaped now, at end of Gordon, see Plate 30) and a quick left on High Road. Continue to Mountain Avenue and turn right. Then right on Glenmore Drive. Drive slowly past the Kelowna Golf and Country Club, the cliff bordering the golf course is a steep rock cliff carved out by a glacier. The cliff has been eroded in places into hoodoo landforms (Plates 12 and 13). The rocks represent feldspathic lava and belong to the Kettle River Group of Eocene age. The base of the cliff can be accessed by a narrow road along the cemetery.

To Varved Clay Stop on KLO Road (7):

Stay on Glenmore Drive which turns into Spall Road. Go to Springfield Road and turn left. Turn right at the next corner onto Cooper Road then right onto Benvoulin Road. Drive slowly past a small white Church, a local historic landmark (it's open, take a look). Continue to the lights at KLO Road and turn left.

After crossing the bridge over Mission Creek and winding up the road, stop at varved clay outcrop on the left(north) side of the road. The road is narrow but there is a small shoulder here. (See Plate 15 and Figure 21).

To Quarry Stop (11):

Continue east on KLO Road to the viewpoint near the top, pull out and park. This spot offers a good view of valley features, and of dipping rocks in distant Okanagan Mountain Park. Keep going and turn right just past McCulloch Pub onto McCulloch Road. The terrain here is hummocky moraine (8) eroded by a meltwater channel in the vicinity of June Springs Road intersection. Go past a golf course to the bridge over KLO (Canyon) Creek. Drive slowly down the hill past till outcrops in the road cut (10). Park at the pull-out just past the bridge, and walk up the trail to a Quarry in the Shuswap rocks (Monashee Gneiss). This is the same stop as Stop 2, in the Hardrock Trail Field Trip (See Appendix B).

After this, continue a short distance up the hill and watch on the left for a large boulder in the trees; this is an erratic.

To Layer Cake Hill Viewpoint (9):

A viewpoint for Gallagher's Canyon, Pinnacle Rock and Layer Cake Hill can be reached by a road through the golf course or along Field Road. This site has received special attention in various parts of this book (refer to Chapter Eight, Figure 22, and Plates 2, 3, 17, 18, 19, 20, 21). There is a lot to see here.

Crawford Falls (30):

Go back onto McCulloch Road, turn left at June Springs Road and go to Stewart Road and turn left. Crawford Falls can be accessed at the end of Stewart Road in Crawford Estates, East Kelowna. A series of waterfalls occur along Bellevue Creek here but viewing them is presently hazardous.

Beach of Glacial Lake Penticton (14)

A spectacular beach ridge can be viewed along the Crawford Escarpment (extension of East Kelowna Escarpment, Figure 19) off of Westridge Road (small undeveloped lot or park here), which joins Crawford Road in Crawford Estates (Plate 23). This represents the highest elevation of glacial Lake Penticton. The beach deposit is up to eight metres thick and overlies sand and gravel of glacial origin exposed in an abandoned gravel pit.

Mt. Boucherie Columns (17)

From Crawford Estates make your way back to Harvey Avenue (Highway 97), perhaps making a stop at the Father Pandosy Historical Site at the corner of Casorso and Benvoulin roads. Also, look at the huge concrete anchor (Plate 35) at Anchor Park at the corner of Ellis and Harvey.

Proceed across Okanagan Lake Bridge (read the account of this famous bridge on pages 108 to 109). Turn left at the second set of lights onto Boucherie Road, turn right on Hudson Road then left on Guidi Road. Turn right on Trevor Drive and continue to the end of the road where there is a turnaround. Park and walk a short distance. Scattered in the forest here are giant rock columns (Plate 37). They are composed of dacite, a volcanic rock that forms part of a volcanic dome that built the mountain. Columnar structures, contorted by folding of the rocks, can be seen high on the east side of the mountain here with binoculars from the turnaround.

Plate 37:
Like a field of toppled columns from some ancient Roman ruins, large blocks of columnar lava composed of dacite litter the forest floor on the slopes of Boucherie Mountain. How did these get here, and where did they come from?

To Glen Canyon (Powers Creek) (20)

Go back down Trevor Drive, turn left on Guidi Road, right on Hudson Road, then right on Boucherie Road. Stay on Boucherie Road all the way to Gellatly Road. An interesting outcrop (19) of conglomerate of the White Lake Formation occurs at the junction of Old Boucherie Road along this route (see page 8, Plate 25, and Stop 6, the Hardrock Trail, Appendix B).

Turn right at Gellatly Road. Observe varved clay and silt of Lake Penticton sediments (19). Turn left at Highway 97 and go through Westbank to Glenrosa Road (Figure 24). Turn right here, go to Weber Road and turn right; proceed to Aberdeen Road and turn right. Go to end of Aberdeen and park. There are several viewpoints of a scenic canyon eroded into sandstone and conglomerate of the White Lake Formation at the end of the trail (see p.32, Plate 5). The trail is steep and occasionally in rough condition.

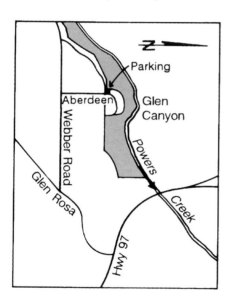

Figure 24: Location of Glen Canyon Regional Park.

APPENDIX B

THE HARDROCK TRAIL FIELD TRIP

by John D. Greenough.

Introduction

The field trip illustrates processes that occur during mountain building events. The event you will study occurred during the Eocene and strongly affected the Kelowna area. Processes illustrated include folding and faulting (stops 1, 4 and 5) igneous activity (stops 1, 3 and 4), metamorphism (stops 2 and 3) and sedimentation (stops 4 and 5). The sedimentary rocks allow us to paint a picture of living conditions in the Okanagan during the Eocene. The trip takes you through East Kelowna, the Okanagan Mission and then along the Kettle Valley Railway bed to Penticton, returning to Kelowna along Highway 97. For those who cannot venture outside of Kelowna stop 3 can be omitted.

Stop 1: Layer Cake Hill Volcanic Rocks.

Proceed out McCulloch Road, past KLO Creek to where a clearing for high-tension power lines provides a spectacular view of layered rocks in Layer Cake Hill on the north side of Mission Creek (see Figure 22 p. 78 and Plate 17, p. 79).

You are standing on Pleistocene sediments that overlie Monashee Gneiss (see Stop 2), and looking at a Middle Eocene "andesitic" lava flow (flows?) of the Marron Formation. This outcrop illustrates that Kelowna was volcanically active approximately 50 million years ago. It also shows that rocks in the area have been folded and faulted since that time.

If you could hold a sample of the rock from across Mission Creek in your hand you would see that it consists of tiny interlocking crystals, the most obvious being grains of plagioclase feldspar. The fine-grained, interlocking texture tells you the rock is a volcanic igneous rock and the feldspars indicate that it is probably an andesite. However, formation of the most prominent feature of the outcrop, its layering, has been the subject of much debate.

Many geologists, including the author initially regarded each layer as a separate lava flow. However, if you look at the outcrop carefully you will see vertical fractures that can be traced across the layers. These fractures are known as columnar jointing which is a common feature in volcanic rocks. It forms when initially hot lava cools, crystallizes and then contracts causing the rock to break into regular five- or six-sided polygonal columns. The observation that the columns cut across the layering indicates that the entire cliff represents a single cooling unit and is not a series of lava flows.

Little (B.N. Church, personal communication, 1993) recognized that the outcrop is probably a single cooling unit and sarcastically proposed that the inclined layers form the threads on the world's largest "Geotectobolt", a plug in the throat of a volcano that screwed itself to the surface! This thesis seems unlikely if for no other reason than that the layers extend back into the cliff. Similar layering occurs within some thick basaltic lava flows. Drill holes through basalts in Hawaii indicate that the layering forms when the crystal-liquid "mush" beneath the hardened upper crust of the lava flow becomes so dense that it begins to sink into the underlying pool of magma. As the "mush" grows downward it tears itself away from the crust at regular time and thickness intervals. The horizontal crack that forms actually sucks liquid out of the crystal mush forming a thin layer of rock between the thick layers that is chemically and mineralogically different in composition. Thus, it is theoretically possible to test this hypothesis for Layer Cake mountain by chemically analyzing the layers. Regardless of how it formed the layering is interesting because it has never been reported from volcanic rocks of this type anywhere else in the world.

Although you cannot see them the rocks you are standing on are metamorphic rocks called gneiss that were strongly affected by the Eocene mountain building event. The metamorphism occurred at least several kilometres down in the earth at the same time that Layer Cake Hill was forming at the surface of the earth. This requires that there is a major Eocene to post-Eocene fault with several kilometres of vertical displacement on it between where you are standing and Layer Cake Mountain. Locally the originally-horizontal layers in Layer Cake Mountain are strongly tilted. Both the folding (bending) and faulting are the result of mountain building forces that acted on the rocks during or after the Eocene.

In summary this stop illustrates three important processes that operate during mountain building events; volcanism, folding and faulting.

Stop 2.
Quarry In Metamorphic Rocks - The Monashee Gneiss.

Proceed back toward Kelowna to a quarry located approximately 100 metres south of the road beside KLO Creek (Figures 19 and 23, p. 68 and 82; Plate 38, p. 152).

Good outcrops of the Monashee Gneiss occur here. Gneisses are metamorphic rocks which are rocks that were changed in form by heat and pressure. A geologist tries to answer several questions when examining metamorphic rocks: 1) what was the original (pre-metamorphism) rock type?; 2) how old was this parent rock?; 3) when was it metamorphosed?; 4) what were the pressure and temperature conditions during metamorphism?, and 5) what do mineral alignments in the rock tell us about the orientation of mountain-building forces during metamorphism?

Pick up a sample of the gneiss. The minerals present reflect the chemical composition (mineralogy) of the original rock as well as the pressure and temperature of metamorphism. The gneiss contains: microcline (K-feldspar) which is white to pink in colour, plagioclase, which is white and very similar in appearance to the microcline, smaller percentages of clear, colourless to light gray quartz, and specs of black minerals which are amphibole and/or biotite. The minerals and mineral proportions are the same as in a granite or its extrusive equivalent rhyolite. Thus, the gneiss may have originally been a granite. Other possible parent rocks include arkose and greywacke which are quartz-poor and feldspar, or clay-rich sandstones (sedimentary rocks) which form from weathering of granites. Some rocks are better than others for determining the pressure and temperature of metamorphism. The minerals present in this rock are not very good. Nevertheless, the presence of amphibole indicates temperatures of at least 450°C with pressures of 2 kilobars (= depths of at least 7 km). Gneisses of all kinds typically form under these conditions.

The age of the parent rock is problematical. As discussed in the text some rocks belonging to this interior metamorphic complex, the Shuswap Complex, are two billion years old. These ages are obtained by radiometric dating of zircons that formed at the time of the parent rock and have survived the effects of metamorphism. Zircons occur in such tiny concentrations in the gneiss that they are not usually observable in hand specimen. Radiometric dating of minerals such as amphibole and biotite that formed during metamorphism indicate that the last metamorphic event to affect the rocks occurred during the Eocene. Note that these rocks may have also been metamorphosed many times prior to the Eocene.

The gneisses differ from granites in that they show bands of light and dark minerals. The bands tend to be horizontal. One process that can form banding is shearing. Imagine rubbing (in one direction only) a wad of putty between your hands. The putty becomes smeared out. The same process affected these rocks. One can determine the sense of shearing by finding eye-shaped crystals of microcline known as augen in some outcrops. The augen tend to have "tails" pointing in opposite directions on their tops and bottoms. Relative motion was in the direction of the tails. These crystals indicate that rocks once above your head moved to the west and those below your feet moved east! The boundary between the rocks that moved west and those that went east occurs under Okanagan Lake. You also observed a portion of this fault at stop 1. Thus movement on the Okanagan fault created the layering now present in the Monashee Gneiss.

Stop 3:
Monashee Gneiss (Amphibolite) Intruded by Granite.

From the quarry, return to Kelowna via McCulloch and KLO Roads, turn left on Gordon Drive and right onto Dehart Road and then left onto Lakeshore Drive. Going up the hill leave Lakeshore Drive and follow Chute Lake Road. Watch on the left for the fire station approximately 1.9 km along Chute Lake Road. Turn left off Chute Lake Road onto Hedeman Road and then right onto the Forestry Service road 0.2 km past the fire station. There are no major turns off the forestry service road until you reach the Kettle Valley Railway bed where you turn right and head toward Naramata.

There are numerous railway cuts through bedrock between the logging road-railway bed junction and Naramata all of which contain Monashee Gneiss (Plate 38). You are encouraged to stop and compare some of these rocks with those examined at Stop 2. Proceed to the southern end of Penticton and take Lee Avenue off Skaha Lake Road. Head east 0.6 km to South Main Street and turn right. Head south along South Main Street for exactly 5 km and stop on the left-hand corner where rocks on the left have been quarried and used to produce the road bed that abuts Skaha Lake (Figure 41). There is lots of room to pull off on the right.

The outcrop illustrates processes that occur during magma intrusion. Granitoid rocks are apparent at the base of the outcrop just before the apex in the corner. These rocks are probably Eocene in age. They intrude Monashee Gneiss

Plate 38: Photograph of Monashee Gneiss along the Kettle Valley Railway bed. The gneiss displays light-colored bands composed dominantly of feldspar and dark bands with abundant amphibole.

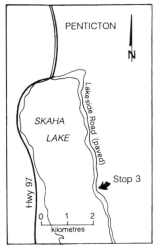

Figure 41

that at this locality is dominantly the metamorphic rock amphibolite as opposed to the "granite gneiss" you saw earlier. The black mineral in the amphibolite is an Iron-rich mineral called hornblende (an amphibole, hence the rock name).

The contact between granite (a light-coloured rock) and amphibolite (a dark rock) is fairly distinct (Plate 39). In contrast to the gneisses you observed earlier the amphibolites at this locality are extremely coarse grained. Heat from the granite caused the surrounding gneiss to be metamorphosed and recrystallized. The coarse grained texture in the amphibolite is a result of volatiles leaving the granite. Volatiles, such as water, are light and they tend to rise and be concentrated in the upper portions of granite intrusions. These volatiles, when they entered the gneiss were capable of moving ions to the surface of growing amphibole crystals. Locally you can see veins where the amphibole crystals are extremely large, even "pegmatitic". These represent channel-ways where volatiles were concentrated as they streamed out of

Plate 39: Photograph showing the sharp contact between granite (bottom of photograph) and coarse-grained amphibolite (top) along Skaha Lake.

the granite. The fluids also enhanced the formation of garnets which occur as abundant, small (< 0.5 cm), round, red mineral grains forming "trails" in the coarse-grained granite commonly about 1 m below the amphibolite (see below for more details on their formation).

Walking south approximately 65 metres around the corner you will find more amphibolites that are not so coarse grained. Close examination shows that some samples also contain a green to dark green mineral which is pyroxene. At this location volatile concentrations were apparently lower and the heat from the intrusion caused amphibole to give up the water in its crystal structure and turn into pyroxene. Very high temperatures, perhaps in excess of 700°C are required for this reaction to take place.

At the same spot there are near-vertical orange to pink granite pegmatites cutting the amphibolites. These may have formed later and resulted from crystallization of the interior of the granite intrusion. Because most minerals in a magma tend to have low volatile contents, fluids such as water tend to build up in the residual liquid as the granite crystallizes. Thus, long after the outer edge of the intrusion had completely crystallized, the interior, which solidified more slowly, had volatiles locally build up to the point where they fractured the solid outer margin of the intrusion. Volatile-rich magma then moved along these fractures creating pegmatite dykes. The large grain sizes reflect the ability of volatiles to enhance crystal growth creating large crystals.

It is not only volatiles that build up in the last drops of liquid to crystallize from a magma. Some elements do not fit in the crystal structure of common silicate minerals such as feldspar and quartz. They become concentrated in the last drops of magma to crystallize. Examples of elements that tend to behave this way are zirconium, tantalum, hafnium, and the rare earth elements (e.g. lanthanum, cerium, lutetium). However, some rare minerals in igneous rocks have an affinity for these elements. For example, garnets accommodate the rare earth elements in their crystal structure. Garnet present in the northern portion of the outcrop is probably related to these processes.

Stop 4:
White Lake Formation and Coal Deposits, Westbank

Proceed north through Penticton, along Highway 97. You may want to briefly examine the Eocene sediments and pyroclastic rocks in a deep roadcut at the northern edge of Summerland in order to compare them with the rocks in Westbank.

Approximately 1.5 km north of the Okanagan Connector exit ramp there is a place to pull off and examine rocks across the road from Gorman Bros. Lumber Ltd. mill (Plate 40). Walk back (south) 190 m from the parking spot.

Rocks at this stop belong to the White Lake Formation and are Middle Eocene in age (approximately 45 million years old). They are a mixture of volcanic rocks and volcanic-rich sediments that filled a caldera stretching from here to the north-

Plate 40: Bedding in White Lake Formation rocks across from the Gorman Bros. Lumber Ltd. lumber mill at Westbank. Prominent beds of sandstone and conglomerate are separated by thin coal beds that tend to be eroded more easily. Tree trunks and root systems displayed in Plate 41 occur in the left-hand portion of the photograph.

ern edge of Kelowna. You passed through another one of these caldera-fill Tertiary basins at Summerland. Calderas form as a result of giant volcanic eruptions that leave behind a large hole in the ground. The sedimentary rocks represent rock material that filled the caldera after its formation. They allow us to paint a picture of Okanagan living conditions during the Eocene event.

Where you are standing, the outcrop is dominated by mudflow deposits composed mostly of coarse-grained conglomerates. The clasts (pieces of earlier rock) in the conglomerate are predominantly volcanic rocks. Reddish brown clasts are probably "andesites" because the white specs (crystals) are plagioclase phenocrysts. Other, light-coloured clasts contain K-feldspar phenocrysts and are probably rhyolites. Dark brown clasts with wisps of lighter material in them are ash-fall lapilli tuffs. The "wisps" of lighter material are lapilli (walnut-sized clots of bubbly magma thrown out of an erupting volcano) that collapsed (became flattened) from the weight of overlying ash. The abundance of volcanic clasts suggests that these are lahars, mudflows that form when snow and ice melt at the top of an erupting volcano. The lahars apparently flowed down a stream valley beyond the base of the volcano because many of the clasts are somewhat rounded and a few are "granitic" and could not have come from a volcano.

Heading north 12 metres, at the upper end of the lahar deposits there is a bed of conglomerate with a concentration of large clasts. This bed (approximately one metre thick) represents the top of a lahar that was worked by water flowing down the stream channel. The flowing water only removed fine-grained material thus

Plate 41: A fossil tree trunk composed of coal. During Eocene time the tree was growing in sand which has been turned into sandstone by the same combination of heat, pressure and time that caused the tree trunk to turn into coal.

increasing the degree of sorting and concentrating the large boulders.

Continuing north 33 metres the sedimentary rocks get finer grained. They are very immature sandstones (greywackes, lithic sandstones and arkoses), and contain abundant volcanic material minimally reworked by stream flow. Some beds may even be unworked ash deposits. These rocks give way to thin (< 20 cm) coal beds between ash-fall and/or sandstone beds. The coal indicates that swamps with abundant plant life periodically developed (Plate 40).

Pacing off another 18 metres you will find coalified roots of trees that can be traced down into soils that started to develop in the volcanic-rich sediments and volcanic ash (Plate 41). Fossils of broad-leaf trees, ferns, and forerunners to modern red wood trees indicate a warm and damp, if not sub-tropical climate.

Ten metres further north there are slightly coarser rocks that contain monolithologic (only one rock type, in this case andesite with feldspar phenocrysts) volcanic clasts. This rock is almost certainly a volcanic ash-fall breccia deposit because the matrix (material between clasts) has the same composition as the clasts.

Apparently living things in the Kelowna area had a difficult time of it during the

Plate 42: White Lake Formation conglomerate showing concretions which have been preferentially weathered (eroded) from the rock face forming "holes".

Eocene. Floods produced raging rivers that periodically swept away or buried life in the swamps. Mudflows (lahars) originating on near-by volcanic edifices buried anything in their path and explosive volcanic eruptions (recorded by the ash beds) regularly smothered everything alive. This was not a nice place to live!

Note that beds in the outcrop are not horizontal (Plate 40). Sedimentologists generally assume that sediments are deposited horizontally. The beds are no longer flat-lying because they were folded toward the end of the Eocene mountain building event.

Stop 5. Conglomerate Cliff on Boucherie Road

Proceed through the business section of Westbank. Turn right at the intersection (lights) with Gellatly Road, and left (head north) onto Boucherie Road upon reaching the lake. Proceed a total of 3.7 km from Highway 97. Watch for a prominent rock cliff containing numerous "holes" on the left-hand side of the road and at the intersection with Old Boucherie Road (Figure 19, p. 68, Plate 25, p. 88 and Plate 42).

These rocks represent more Middle Eocene conglomerate deposits but they are different from those at Stop 4. They show much better sorting (fine grains have been separated from coarse grains by running water) and at this outcrop the dominant clast type is granitic. Other clasts of lesser importance include yellow-brown andesite clasts and foliated (mineral grains are lined up) granite gneiss pebbles. The source for these clasts has not been determined but it is likely that they did not come from the Kelowna area. These are river gravel deposits brought in by a major river flowing through the caldera complex. Notice how well sorted and well bedded they are compared to the rocks at stop 4.

Study of the mineral material cementing the rocks together indicates the origin of the holes in the outcrop. Inspection of freshly blasted rocks at the base of the cliff reveals several oval areas where the rocks are lighter in colour. These spots react vigorously to dilute hydrochloric acid (HCl) indicating the presence of calcite as a cementing agent. Away from these oval spots, which are referred to as concretions the rock does not react to acid. Apparently soon after the gravels were deposited, groundwater percolating through the sediment started depositing calcite at random locations. In the millions of years following this early episode of cementation quartz dissolved in groundwater cemented the remainder of the rock together. Over the past 10,000 years, rainwater, which is mildly acidic as a result of absorbing CO_2 from the atmosphere, dissolved away the calcite holding the concretions together. Once the cementing agent was removed the original sand and gravel simply fell out of the rock face leaving the prominent holes.

Note that bedding (layering in the rocks) is inclined because, just as at the last stop, the rocks were folded toward the end of the Eocene mountain building event.

Summary and Conclusions

Mountain-building processes result in the formation of igneous, sedimentary and metamorphic rocks as well as folding and faulting activity. During the Eocene the Kelowna area was affected by a major mountain building event. You saw andesitic lava probably trapped in the throat of a volcano at the first stop and ash-fall deposits at stop 4. The lahar mudflows at stop 4 can also be regarded as volcanic deposits. Stop 3 illustrated intrusive igneous processes which resulted in metamorphism and recrystallization of amphibolites making up the Monashee Gneiss as well as granite pegmatite formation.

Sedimentary processes were represented at stops 4 and 5. Thin coal seams at stop 4 are products of the accumulation of plant material in swamps and bogs. Conglomerate at stop 5 indicates that a major river flowed through the area during the Eocene. Fossils in the sediments suggest a warm, humid, perhaps subtropical climate. Periodic flash floods, mud flows (lahars) and explosive volcanism made life in the Okanagan difficult during the Eocene.

Metamorphic rocks at stops 2 and 3 contain minerals that formed at depths of perhaps 7 kilometres and temperatures of at least 450°C. These temperatures were the result of regional heating during the mountain building event. The foliation in the gneisses (banding and mineral alignment) indicates that rocks that occurred above the gneisses moved toward the west.

Rocks at stops 1, 4 and 5 were folded during mountain building. Faulting occurred, especially toward the end of the event. At stop 1 the juxtaposition of Eocene volcanic rocks (formed at the surface of the earth) and metamorphic rocks (formed simultaneously perhaps 7 or more kilometres down) suggests that 7 kilometres of vertical movement occurred along the Okanagan fault. The foliation in the Monashee Gneiss indicates that the fault was a low angle fault and that rocks to the west of Okanagan Lake moved dozens if not hundreds of kilometres to the west unearthing the Monashee Gneisses in the east.

All photos in Appendix B were taken by John D. Greenough.

APPENDIX C

GEOFACTS OF KELOWNA

1. Maximum elevation of glacial Lake Penticton is 457.2 metres (1,500 feet)

2. Maximum depth of Okanagan Lake is 232 metres (761 feet), off Whiskey Island, five kilometres north of Okanagan Centre.

3. Maximum thickness of glacial and post-glacial sediment fill in Okanagan Lake is 750m (2,460 feet).

4. Elevation of the bedrock floor beneath Lake Okanagan at the deepest is -640 metres (-2,100 feet).

5. Okanagan Lake is approximately 120 kilometres long and averages about 3.5 kilometres in width.

6. Elevation of Lake Okanagan is an average of 342 metres (1,123 feet).

7. Maximum water level fluctuation for Lake Okanagan (1943-1979) is from 0 to 1.68 metres (5.5 feet).

8. Oldest rock in the area is the Monashee Gneiss, 2.0 billion years or older. Also the oldest rock in British Columbia.

9. Youngest rock in the area is the Lambly Creek Basalt, 0.762 million years, just west of the Okanagan Bridge.

10. Highest point of land in Kelowna area: Little White Mountain, elevation 2,171 metres (7,122 feet). Terminus of the Crawford Trail.

11. Relief on the bedrock surface in the Okanagan Valley from the highest point (Little White Mountain) to the lowest beneath the lake is 2,814 metres, almost double that of the Grand Canyon in Arizona at 1,600 metres.

12. The last glacier that occupied the area is the Fraser Glacier that persisted for 9,000 years from 19,000 to 10,000 years Before Present. This glacier was at least 3,000 metres (10,000 feet) thick along the centre line of Okanagan Lake.

An earlier glacier referred to as the Okanagan Centre glaciation occupied the region about 50,000 years ago. There are indirect regional indications that there have been six glacial episodes dating to over one million years ago.

13. Sixty million years ago, in the early part of the Tertiary Period of geologic time, there was substantial volcanic activity in the Kelowna area.

14. The Okanagan fault, a major break in the earth's crust, has been found to extend to a depth of approximately twenty kilometres.

15. The Okanagan Valley along which the Okanagan fault occurs is at least 200 kilometres long.

16. The upland that flanks both sides of the Okanagan Valley is known as the Thompson Plateau on the west and the Okanagan Highland on the east.

17. The Thompson Plateau is capped in places by nearly flat-lying volcanic rocks of basaltic composition, ten to twenty million years old.

APPENDIX D

GLOSSARY OF TERMS

AIR PHOTO: A photograph of the earth's surface taken from the air. It is usually a vertical view, and one of a series of photos taken from an aircraft flying a systematic pattern at a given altitude in order to obtain continuous photo coverage for mapping purposes.

ALLUVIAL FAN: A fan-shaped deposit of fluvial sand and gravel, usually located at the mouth of a tributary valley; a type of floodplain.

ANDESITE: A dark-colored, fine-grained igneous rock that is the extrusive form of diorite. It is between basalt and rhyolite in chemical composition and was named after the Andes Mountains in South America where it is common.

BASALT: A form of dark-colored lava, composed chiefly of calcium feldspar and pyroxene. Basalt and its coarse-grained equivalent, gabbro, are the principal kinds of rocks that form the crust beneath the deep oceans.

BATHOLITH: (i) A stock-shaped or shield-shaped mass (of igneous rock) intruded as the fusion of older formations. On removal of its rock cover and on continued denudation, this mass holds its diameter or grows broader to unknown depths. (ii) A body of intrusive rock, with the general characteristics of stocks or plutons, but of much larger size than is generally attributed to stocks or bosses.

BEACH: The gently sloping shore of a body of water that is washed by waves and usually composed of loose sandy or gravelly material.

BEDDING: Collective term signifying the existence of beds or laminae. WELL BEDDED indicates beds are immediately apparent, clearly defined and can be easily traced across the deposit; POORLY BEDDED means beds are only discernible after careful scrutiny, or bedding planes are discontinuous; MODERATELY BEDDED is intermediate between the other two.

BEDROCK: Solid rock, usually older than Quaternary (except rock formed by cooling of lava); either exposed at the land surface or underlying surficial deposits or regolith of varying thickness.

BLACK CHERNOZEMIC: Neutral to basic soils with substantial organic matter accumulation in the surface layer (horizon); black in color.

BLANKET: A mantle of surficial material, thicker than about 1 metre, that reflects the topography of the bedrock or older surficial material upon which it rests although minor details of that topography may be masked.

BOULDER: (i) A rock fragment larger than 256 mm intermediate diameter (Wentworth scale). (ii) Somewhat rounded rock fragment larger than 256 mm intermediate diameter.

BROWN CHERNOZEMIC: Neutral to basic soils with slight organic matter accumulation in the surface layer and developed under climatically dry grassland; brown in color.

BURIED VALLEY: A valley which has been filled by unconsolidated deposits, such as glacial drift.

CALDERA: A large basin-shaped volcanic depression, more or less circular or cirque-like in form, the diameter of which is many times greater than that of the included volcanic vent or vents, no matter what the steepness of the walls or form of the floor. Classified into three major types: explosion calderas, collapse calderas, and erosion calderas.

CIRQUE: A rounded recess in a mountain formed by glacial erosion, with steep head and side walls, and a relatively gently-sloping floor that is commonly a basin with a small lake and terminated downvalley by a convex break of slope. Cirques range in diameter from a few hundred metres to several kilometres. They occur at the head of, or cut into the flanks of, glacial troughs. Cirque glacier is a glacier that occupies a cirque.

CLASTIC SEDIMENTS: Sediments consisting of detrital particles derived by mechanical breakdown of rocks.

CLAY: (i) A rock or mineral fragment of any composition having a diameter less than 1/256 mm (4 micrometers) (Wentworth scale). (ii) A finely crystalline hydrous silicate of aluminum, iron, manganese, magnesium, and other metals belonging to the phyllosilicate group, such as kaolinite, montmorillonite, bentonite, and vermiculite; known as CLAY MINERALS.

COBBLE: (i) A rock fragment between 64 and 256 mm intermediate diameter (Wentworth scale). (ii) Rounded and subrounded rock fragments between 62 and 256 mm intermediate diameter.

COLLUVIAL FAN: A fan-shaped mass of sediments deposited by colluvial processes, most commonly debris flows.

CONTACTS (STRATIGRAPHIC): The surfaces that separate a stratigraphic unit from overlying and underlying units; may be sharp or gradational, horizontal or inclined, planar or wavy.

CORDILLERAN ICE SHEET: The complex of icefields, mountain icecaps and piedmont glaciers that covered much of the Canadian Cordillera, including all of British Columbia, during the Fraser Glaciation for example.

DACITE: A volcanic rock with a finely crystalline or glassy texture, composed of plagioclase feldspar, quartz, pyroxene or hornblende or both with minor biotite and sanidine. It is the extrusive equivalent of quartz diorite.

DARK BROWN CHERNOZEMIC: Neutral to basic soils with moderate organic matter accumulation in the surface layer and developed under grassland; dark brown in color.

DEBRIS AVALANCHE: Rapid downslope movement on steep slopes of saturated soil and/or surficial material, commonly including vegetative debris; a very rapid to extremely rapid debris flow.

DEBRIS FLOW: Rapid flow of a slurry of saturated debris, including some or all of soil, surficial material, weathered rock, mud, boulders, and vegetative debris. A general designation for all types of rapid downslope flow, including mudflows, rapid earthflows, and debris torrents.

DEBRIS TORRENT: A variety of debris flow that includes little fines (silt and clay) and that follows a pre-existing stream channel.

DEPOSIT: An accumulation of earth material resulting from naturally-occurring physical, chemical, or organic processes.

DELTA: An accumulation of stream-transported sediments deposited where a stream enters a body of water. The landform is flat or very gently sloping, triangular or fan-shaped in plan, and consists of fluvial (alluvial) gravel, sand, silt and/or clay.

DIATOMACEOUS EARTH: A friable earthy deposit composed of nearly pure silica and consisting essentially of the frustules of microscopic plants called diatoms.

DRIFT: (i) All sediments deposited by glacier ice or by glacial meltwater. (ii) Includes till, glaciofluvial and glaciolacustrine materials.

DRUMLIN: A streamlined hill or ridge of till or other drift, with a long axis that parallels the direction of flow of a former glacier; generally the upstream end is widest and highest, and the drumlin tapers in the downflow direction.

DYSTRIC BRUNISOL: Acidic, reddish to yellowish, strongly weathered soils developed under climatically moist, forested conditions.

EOLIAN MATERIALS: Sediments transported and deposited by wind.

EROSION: The loosening and removal of materials by wind, moving water, weathering, gravity, and glacier ice.

ERRATIC: Boulders or smaller clasts of rock types that are dissimilar to underlying bedrock and transported to their present location by glacier ice.

ESCARPMENT: A steep slope that is usually of great lateral extent compared to its height, such as the risers of river terraces and steep faces associated with stratified rocks or surficial materials.

ESKER: A sinuous ridge of sand and gravel resulting from deposition by meltwater in a tunnel beneath or within a glacier or ice sheet. The ridges generally trend at right angles to a glacier margin, and the sand and gravel may be covered by till or glaciolacustrine sediments.

EUTRIC BRUNISOL: Neutral to basic, weakly weathered soils developed under climatically dry forested conditions.

FAN: (i) An accumulation of detrital material in the shape of a low-angle cone, usually at the point where a stream emerges from a valley onto a plain. (ii) A sector of a cone with gradient not steeper than 15°. (See alluvial fan, colluvial fan.)

FAULT: Faults are fractures in the earth along which rocks on one side of the fracture have moved relative to rocks on the other side. Faults are further classified on the basis of the kind of movement that has occurred; vertical movement include normal and reverse faults; horizontal movements are strike-slip faults; low angle faults are thrust faults.

FELDSPAR: A group of closely related minerals composed of silica, oxygen, aluminum and one or more of potassium, sodium and calcium. Examples include orthocalse and plagioclase.

FLOODPLAIN: Level or very gently sloping surface bordering a river that has been formed by river erosion and deposition; it is usually subject to flooding, and is underlain by fluvial sediments; similar to alluvial plain.

FLUTINGS: (i) Smooth, straight furrows, parallel to ice-flow direction, and formed in bedrock by glacial abrasion. (ii) Smooth, straight, shallow furrows, parallel to ice-flow direction, in till or other drift.

FLUVIAL: Pertaining to streams and rivers; similar to alluvial.

FOLD: A bend in strata or any planar structure. Upfolds are called anticlines and downfolds are called synclines. Overturned fold is a fold in which one or the other limb has been turned upside down.

FRASER GLACIATION: Name given to the most recent Pleistocene glaciation in British Columbia and adjacent Washington State; equivalent to Late Wisconsinan Glaciation.

GEOLOGICAL STRUCTURE: The three dimensional arrangement of geological contacts and discontinuities, such as bedding, stratification, joints, faults, dikes, plutons, folds.

GEOMORPHOLOGY: The study of the origin of landforms, the processes whereby they are formed, and the materials of which they consist.

GEOMORPHOLOGICAL HISTORY: The evolution of landforms and landscapes, surface materials, and changes with time in geomorphological processes.

GEOMORPHOLOGICAL PROCESSES: Dynamic actions or events that occur at the earth's surface due to application of natural forces resulting from gravity, temperature changes, freezing and thawing, chemical reactions, seismic shaking, and the agencies of wind and moving water, ice and snow. Where and when a force exceeds the strength of the earth material, the material is changed by deformation, translocation, or chemical reactions.

GLACIAL ABRASION: The scouring action of particles embedded in glacier ice.

GLACIAL HISTORY: The time-sequence of glaciations, glacial advances and recessions.

GLACIAL LAKE: (i) A lake that derives much or all of its water from the melting of glacier ice, i.e., fed by meltwater. (ii) A lake that is dammed by a glacier or resting on glacial ice.

GLACIER: A body of ice formed by the compaction and recrystallization of snow, that has definite lateral limits, and with motion in a definite direction.

GLACIER OUTBURST FLOOD: A catastrophic flood that results from the collapse of an ice-dam and rapid drainage of a glacial lake.

GLACIOFLUVIAL: Pertaining to the channelized flow of glacier meltwater (meltwater streams), and deposits and landforms formed by meltwater streams.

GLACIOFLUVIAL MATERIALS: Sediments that exhibit clear evidence of having been deposited by glacial meltwater streams either directly in front of, or in contact with, glacier ice; most commonly sands and gravels.

GLACIOLACUSTRINE: Pertaining to glacial lakes.

GLACIOLACUSTRINE MATERIALS: Sediments deposited in or along the margins of glacial lakes; primarily fine sand, silt and clay settled from suspension or from subaqueous gravity flows (turbidity currents), and including coarser sediments (e.g., ice-rafted boulders) released by the melting of floating ice; also includes littoral sediments (e.g., beach sand or gravel) accumulated as a result of wave action.

GLEYSOLIC: Mottled and gleyed soils developed under high water table and saturated conditions.

GNEISS: A foliated, coarse-grained, high-grade metamorphic rock characterized by alternating layers of dark and light-coloured minerals that commonly show flow folding, i.e. typical of rock deformation under plastic conditions.

GRANITE: A light colored, coarse grained crystalline igneous rock that is made up mostly of plagioclase, potassium feldspar, and quartz; but which may also contain a little mica or hornblende.

GRAVEL: (i) An accumulation of rounded pebbles. (ii) An accumulation of rounded particles that includes at least two of the size classes represented by pebbles, cobbles and boulders; may include interstitial sand.

GRAY LUVISOL: Forested soils with a thick, eluviated (leached) surface layer underlain by a clay accumulation subsurface layer.

GULLY: A small valley or ravine, longer than wide, and typically from a few metres to a few tens of metres across.

GULLY EROSION: Formation of gullies in surficial materials and/or bedrock by a variety of processes including erosion by running water; erosion as a result of weathering and the impact of falling rocks, debris slides, debris flows and other types of mass movement; and erosion by snow avalanches.

HOLOCENE EPOCH: The most recent interval of geological time; from approximately 10,000 years ago to present; similar to postglacial time and also called Recent.

HUMMOCKS: Steep-sided hillocks and hollows, non-linear and chaotically-arranged, and with rounded or irregular cross-profiles; slopes are between 15 and 35° (26-70%) on surficial materials and between 15 and 90° (more than 26%) on bedrock.

HUMMOCKY MORAINE: A moraine consisting of an apparently random assemblage of knobs, kettles, hummocks, ridges, and depressions.

HYDROLOGY: The scientific study of the distribution and characteristics of water at and close to the earth's surface.

HYDROLOGIC FEATURES: Refers to water-related features visible at the land surface, such as stream channels, seepage zones, springs, and soil moisture, including soil moisture characteristics as deduced from vegetation characteristics.

HYPSITHERMAL: Early to mid-Holocene warm interval; also referred to as "xerothermic interval" and "climatic optimum"; in British Columbia, warm interval commenced at or shortly after deglaciation; dates reported for end of warm interval are not consistent, and vary from about 6000 to about 2500 years ago.

ICE-DISINTEGRATION MORAINE: A moraine resulting from the accumulation of ablation till and other drift on top of stagnant ice; similar to hummocky moraine and ablation moraine.

ICE-CONTACT: Pertains to sediments deposited against, on top of, or in tunnels underneath a glacier or ice sheet.

ICE-RAFTED STONES: Stones dropped into glaciolacustrine and glaciomarine sediments from melting icebergs; also called dropstones.

ICE SHEET: A continental-scale, more or less continuous cover of land ice that spreads outward in all directions and is not confined by underlying topography.

IGNEOUS ROCKS: Rocks formed from the solidification of molten magma. Those which formed below the earth's surface are coarsely crystalline and are called intrusive rocks. When intrusive rocks are uplifted and uncovered by erosion they are called plutons or batholiths. Igneous rocks that solidified at the earth's surface are called extrusive or volcanic rocks; they are finely crystalline.

INTRUSIVE ROCKS: See igneous rocks.

KAME: Irregular or conical hillocks composed chiefly of sand and gravel; formed by deposition of meltwater-transported sediments in contact with (against, within, or upon) stagnant glacier ice; a type of glaciofluvial deposit.

KAME DELTA: A delta of sand and gravel constructed in contact with (against or on top of) glacier ice; commonly a conspicuous terrace-like landform bounded by a steep ice-contact face or by hummocky collapsed ground; a type of glaciofluvial deposit.

KETTLE: A closed depression or hollow in glacial drift which has resulted from melting of a buried or partly buried mass of glacier ice; common in glaciofluvial deposits.

KETTLE OUTWASH: Outwash plain with kettles.

LACUSTRINE: Pertaining to a lake.

LACUSTRINE MATERIALS: Sediments that have settled from suspension or underwater gravity flows in lakes; also includes littoral sediments (e.g., beach gravels) accumulated as a result of wave action.

LANDFORM: Any physical, recognizable form or feature of the earth's surface, having a characteristic shape, and produced by natural processes.

LANDSCAPE: A particular part of the earth's surface, such as can be seen from a vantage point or examined on an air photo, and the various landforms and other physical features which together make up the field of view.

LANDSLIDE: A general term for the downslope movement of large masses of earth material and the resulting landforms.

LANDSLIDE SCAR: The part of a slope exposed or visibly modified by detachment and downslope movement of a landslide; usually lies upslope from the displaced landslide material; commonly a steep, concave slope.

LITTLE ICE AGE: The interval of relatively cool/moist climate that occurred during the 15th to 19th centuries and during which most mountain glaciers attained their greatest size since the last Pleistocene glaciation; see also Neoglaciation.

LOESS: A homogeneous, nonstratified, not indurated, yellowish to buff-coloured wind borne deposit consisting predominantly of silt-sized particles with subordinate amounts of fine sand and clay, porous and permeable, commonly with incipient vertical joints.

MAGMA: Molten material, mainly derived from the mantle and intruded into the crust, from which igneous rocks are formed.

MASS MOVEMENT: A general term for downslope gravitational movement of earth materials by processes such as rockfall and debris slides.

MASS WASTING: (i) A general term for a variety of processes, including weathering and erosion, that together effect reduction of slopes and lowering of the land surface. (ii) See mass movement.

MASSIVE: Rocks or sediments without stratification, bedding, flow-banding, or foliation.

MATRIX: The groundmass of smaller grains in which larger particles are supported.

MEANDERING CHANNEL: Refers to a stream channel characterized by a series of freely developing curves, bends, loops, turns or windings in the course of a stream.

MELTWATER CHANNEL: A channel or a valley formed or followed by a glacial meltwater stream; according to their position, they are divided into ice-marginal (lateral) channels, subglacial channels, etc.

MIDDEN: A heap or stratum of refuse (broken tools, shells, ashes, etc.) normally found on the site of an ancient settlement.

MORAINE: (i) A landform that consists of till or, less commonly, of other drift; it exhibits a variety of shapes, ranging from plains to mounds and ridges, that are initial constructional forms independent of underlying bedrock or older materials. (ii) See till.

MORAINE RIDGES: Refers to major moraines, such as end moraines, lateral moraines, and recessional moraines, and small moraines, such as washboard moraine.

MORPHOLOGY: The three-dimensional shape or geometry of a landform or other feature.

NEOGLACIAL INTERVAL, NEOGLACIATION: The episode of relatively cool/moist climate during the later part of the Holocene Epoch during which glaciers were more extensive than during the earlier part of the Holocene (see Hypsithermal). In British Columbia, at least three Neoglacial advances have been recognized, approximately 6000-5000, 3400-2200 years B.P. and since about 1000 years ago; the most recent of these intervals is the Little Ice Age.

ORGANIC MATERIALS: Sediments formed by the accumulation of decaying vegetative matter, such as peat.

OROGENY: The process by which structures within fold-belt mountainous areas were formed. Includes thrusting, folding, and faulting in the outer and higher layers, and plastic flow, metamorphism and plutonism in the inner and deeper layers.

OUTWASH: Glaciofluvial sediments deposited by glacial meltwater downstream from a glacier.

OUTWASH PLAIN: A flat or very gently sloping surface underlain by glaciofluvial sediments.

PALEOZOIC ERA: The span of geological time from 570 to 230 million years ago, i.e. the beginning of the Cambrian to the end of the Permian Periods.

PEBBLE: (i) A rock fragment between 2 and 64 mm intermediate diameter; (Wentworth scale). (ii) A rounded rock fragment between 2 and 64 mm diameter.

PEDOLOGICAL: Pertaining to the study of the formation and development of soil at the land surface.

PERMEABLE: A material through which water can pass.

PHYSIOGRAPHY: Pertains to the factors that influence the development of landforms or a landscape, such as relief and topography, bedrock geology and structure, and geomorphological history.

PHYSIOGRAPHIC REGION: An area of similar relief and topography, bedrock geology and structure, geomorphological history and landforms.

PIPING: Subsurface erosion of particulate materials by flowing water, resulting in the formation of underground caves and conduits and the development of collapse-depressions at the land surface.

PITTED OUTWASH (PLAIN): An outwash plain with kettles.

PLACER DEPOSIT: A surficial mineral deposit formed by mechanical concentration of mineral particles from weathered debris. Common types are beach placers and stream placers. Heavy minerals are usually concentrated, like magnetite, limonite, garnet, gold, rutile, platinum and cassiterite.

PLAIN: (i) A level or very gently sloping planar surface with gradient up to 3 degrees (5%); local relief is less than 1 m. (ii) An extensive region of comparatively smooth and level or gently undulating land, having few or no prominent surface irregularities, and usually at a low elevation with reference to surrounding areas.

PLATE TECTONICS: A theory of global tectonics in which the lithosphere is divided into a number of plates whose pattern of horizontal movement is that of torsionally rigid bodies that interact with one another at their boundaries, causing seismic and tectonic activity along these boundaries.

PLEISTOCENE: An epoch of the Quaternary Period, after the Pliocene of the Tertiary and before the Holocene; characterized by repeated glacial and non-glacial intervals; also, the corresponding worldwide series of deposits.

PLUTON: Pertaining to a body of intrusive and igneous origin, commonly granite or granodiorite.

PODZOLIC: Reddish and brownish forested soils developed under cool and moist conditions with subsurface layers enriched with iron and aluminum sesquioxides and organic matter. A layer of forest litter is usually present on the soil surface and is often underlain by a thin, whitish leached mineral layer.

PORE SPACES: The spaces between the particles of detrital sediments that are not occupied by mineral matter.

POROSITY: The amount of pore space present, expressed as a percentage of the total volume of the material.

POSTGLACIAL: Pertaining to the time interval since the disappearance of glaciers or an ice sheet from a particular area; similar to Holocene Epoch.

PRECAMBRIAN: The span of time from the origin of the Earth to the beginning of the Cambrian Period; i.e. about 4,000 million years.

PYROCLASTIC SEDIMENTS (MATERIALS): A general term applied to detrital volcanic materials that have been explosively or aerially ejected from a volcanic vent, such as ash and cinders.

QUATERNARY PERIOD: The most recent geological time period; subdivided into the Pleistocene and Holocene (Recent) Epochs; currently defined as beginning about 1.6 million years ago.

QUATERNARY DEPOSITS (MATERIALS): Sediments deposited during the Quaternary Period; similar to surficial materials.

RADIOMETRIC (AGE) DATING: A method of determining the age of rocks and minerals by measuring the ratio of radioactive parent elements and the stable daughter elements into which they decay.

REGOSOLIC: Young soils which do not exhibit soil layers typical of soil formation.

RICHTER SCALE: Refers to an earthquake magnitude scale based on the response to ground motion of a "standard seismograph" located 100 kilometres from an epicenter. The scale is logarithmic, meaning that the recorded amplitude of a magnitude 7.0 earthquake is ten times stronger than a magnitude 6.0 earthquake, one hundred times stronger than a magnitude 5.0, and so on.

RIFT VALLEY: An elongated valley formed by the depression of a block of the earth's crust between two faults or fault zones of approximately parallel strike, a graben.

RIVER TERRACE: A more or less flat surface bounded downslope by a scarp and resulting from fluvial erosion and deposition. Same as fluvial terraces and alluvial terraces.

ROCHE MOUTONNÉE: A knob of rock with a whale-back form, the long axis of which is oriented parallel to former ice flow, and having a smooth, glacially-abraded stoss (up-flow) slope and a much steeper and rougher, glacially-plucked lee slope.

ROCK SLIDE: Rapid or slow downslope movement of a large mass of rock by sliding along one or more well defined surfaces of rupture.

SAND: A detrital particle having a diameter in the range of 1/16 to 2 mm.

SEDIMENTARY ROCKS: Rocks resulting from the consolidation of loose sediment that has accumulated in layers, or strata. The sediments may be produced by mechanical means (fragments of older rocks transported from a source and deposited in water or from air), chemical means (precipitates from solution) or organic means (e.g. limestones constructed from the remains or secretions of plants and animals).

SEEPAGE ZONE: An area where soil is saturated due to emerging ground water.

SEISMIC: Pertaining to earthquakes.

SILT: A detrital particle having a diameter in range of 1/256 to 1/16 mm (0.004 to 0.0625 mm).

SINKHOLES: A funnel shaped depression in the land surface that communicates with a subterranean passage developed by solution; common in limestone and karst regions: also applied to similar features caused by piping.

SLOPE FAILURE: Rupture and collapse, or flow, of surficial materials, soil, or bedrock due to shear stress exceeding shear strength of the material.

SLOPE STABILITY: Pertains to the susceptibility of slope to landslides and the likelihood of slope failure.

SLUMP: A landslide characterized by a shearing and rotary movement of a cohesive mass of rock or earth along a concave, upwardly curved slip surface; rotational slump.

SLUMP-EARTHFLOW: A complex landslide displaying characteristics of a slump in its headward zone, and characteristics of an earthflow in its downslope zone.

SLUMP STRUCTURE: Warped or faulted bedding or stratification within a deposit, resulting from downslope movement due to gravity since deposition.

SOIL: The natural medium for growth of land plants; the result of the combined effects of physical, chemical and biological processes.

SOIL (ENGINEERING): See surficial materials, Quaternary materials.

SOIL DRAINAGE: Refers to the rapidity and extent of water removal from the soil in relation to additions, especially by surface runoff and by percolation downwards through the soil.

SOLONETZIC: Soils containing high proportions of sodium, magnesium and other salts.

STAGNANT ICE: Part of a glacier or ice sheet within which ice is no longer flowing; stationary ice; usually melting by downwasting.

STEEP SLOPE: A planar surface steeper than about 35° (70%).

STEREOPAIR: Two adjacent photos from a flight line; can be viewed simultaneously under a stereoscope to obtain a three-dimensional image.

STRIAE, STRIATIONS: Fine cut lines (scratches) on the surface of bedrock or clasts formed by glacial abrasion; oriented parallel to former ice-flow direction; more than one ice-flow directions may be represented by criss-crossing striae.

SUBDUCTION: A process of one lithospheric plate descending beneath another. A related concept was originally used by Alpine geologists.

SURFACE EXPRESSION: Refers to small topographic features and landforms that are not usually shown adequately on a topographic map, and to the relation of a surficial material to the underlying surface; terminology, such as "terrace", "cone", is defined in a non-genetic sense.

SURFICIAL DEPOSITS (MATERIAL): Relatively young, non-lithified sediments, usually of Quaternary age; usually classified as to their genesis, hence fluvial sediments, colluvium, glaciolacustrine sediments, etc.

SURFICIAL GEOLOGY: Geology of surficial deposits.

SURFICIAL GEOLOGY MAP: A map that shows the types and distribution of surficial materials in a chronostratigraphic framework.

TALUS: Angular rock fragments accumulated at the foot of a steep rock slope and being the product of successive rock falls; a type of colluvium.

TERRACE: Any relatively level or gently inclined surface, generally less broad than a plain, and bounded along one side by a steeper descending slope or scarp and along the other by a steeper ascending slope or scarp.

TERRAIN: (i) A comprehensive term to describe a tract of landscape being studied with respect to its natural features. (ii) Pertains to maps showing the origin of surficial material, material texture, surface expression, present day geomorphological (geological) processes, and related features.

TERRAIN ANALYSIS: The process of terrain mapping and interpretation or assessment of terrain conditions for a specific purpose such as construction of logging roads or urban expansion.

TERRANE: Area of the lithosphere distinguished by a certain assemblage of rock types.

TILL: Material deposited by glaciers and ice sheets without modification by any other agent of transportation. Includes basal till, lodgement till, ablation till, flow till, supraglacial till, meltout till.

TILL PLAIN: A level or gently undulating surface underlain by till.

UNCONFORMITY: A substantial break or gap in the geologic record where a rock unit is overlain by another that is not next in stratigraphic succession, such as an interruption in the continuity of a depositional sequence of sedimentary rocks or a break between eroded igneous rocks and younger sedimentary rocks.

VALLEY FILL: Surficial materials that fill or partly fill a valley.

VALLEY GLACIER: Glacier confined by valley sides; usually much longer than broad.

VARVES: Sedimentary beds or laminae where annual layers are distinguishable; most commonly present in glaciolacustrine and lacustrine sediments.

VENEER: A thin mantle of surficial material that does not mask the topographic irregularities of the surface upon which it rests; ranges in thickness from 10 cm to about 1 m.

VOLCANIC ASH: Pyroclastic material less than 2 mm in size.

WATER TABLE: The upper surface of the zone of groundwater saturation in permeable rocks or surficial materials.

WEATHERING: The decomposition and disintegration of bedrock *in situ* due to chemical and physical processes.

APPENDIX E

INDEX

Geology of the Kelowna Area

Geology of the Kelowna Area